Atlantis

Stephen Shaw

Atlantis

Stephen Shaw's Books

Visit the website: www.i-am-stephen-shaw.com

I Am contains spiritual and mystical teachings from enlightened masters that point the way to love, peace, bliss, freedom and spiritual awakening.

Heart Song takes you on a mystical adventure into creating your reality and manifesting your dreams, and reveals the secrets to attaining a fulfilled and joyful life.

They Walk Among Us is a love story spanning two realities. Explore the mystery of the angels. Discover the secrets of Love Whispering.

The Other Side explores the most fundamental question in each reality. What happens when the physical body dies? Where do you go? Expand your awareness. Journey deep into the Mystery.

Reflections offers mystical words for guidance, meditation and contemplation. Open the book anywhere and unwrap your daily inspiration.

5D is the Fifth Dimension. Discover ethereal doorways hidden in the fabric of space-time. Seek the advanced mystical teachings.

Star Child offers an exciting glimpse into the future on earth. The return of the gods and the advanced mystical teachings. And the ultimate battle of light versus darkness.

The Tribe expounds the joyful creation of new Earth. What happened after the legendary battle of Machu Picchu? What is Christ consciousness? What is Ecstatic Tantra?

The Fractal Key reveals the secrets of the shamans. This handbook for psychonauts discloses the techniques and practices used in psychedelic healing and transcendent journeys.

I am going to tell you a story. An ancient story. A magical history that will resonate in your soul. A history ingrained in your deepest consciousness, in your myths and mysteries. For many of you, it will explain your innermost feelings, longings, reveries and dreams. For some of you, it may evoke a profound and beautiful déjà vu.

I am your narrator. We have met before. As we drift through the twists and turns of this story, you may begin to remember me. I will reveal myself later on. Now, pay close attention. Take your time. There is much to absorb. Relaxing deep breath … exhale. Let's start at the beginning.

In the beginning there was Something and Nothing. By choosing to Love, the Something created and expanded, manifesting Itself as Life. The Nothing, by its nature, could not create. As time went by, the Something became vastly more powerful than the Nothing, resulting in the Nothing becoming a constricted border around the Something. Nothing cannot create Something. Something has always existed. Nothing exists alongside Something. Nothing cannot destroy Something. It is the nature of Something to create Something. Something will always exist.

The Something is usually called God or the Source.

The Source is the Unmanifested Consciousness also known as the Mind of God.

The Mind of God looked upon the dark waters of potentiality, resonated the Word, and manifested Creation. Light cascaded through the darkness. The Mind of God became visible as All That Is.

All Creation is the Thought of God.

All Thoughts of God are positioned in layered multi-dimensional realities. All points of consciousness are journeying toward God. The Source manifests countless dimensions and infinite realities – the Out-Breath, the act of creation. All of creation flows back to the Source – the In-Breath, the return and dissolution. This is the flow of Life.

The first creation was infinite multi-dimensions. These are not places, rather they are vibrations or radiances of the Light. You are currently surrounded and permeated with these multi-dimensions.

The second creation was innumerable spiritual beings populating the multi-dimensions. These are aspects of God. All in different stages, on a journey of ascending consciousness, gradually returning to the Source.

The third creation was the Elohim, ethereal beings dedicated to creation of physical worlds. They are responsible for creating universes, galaxies, stars and planets (collectively known as Gaia). They are also responsible for creating physical species to inhabit the various galaxies.

The Elohim had interesting and exciting projects. Physical worlds represent the most dense and concentrated aspects of Reality. Physical worlds offer unique challenges and immediate growth opportunities. There is a vast array of universes, galaxies, stars and planets.

Advanced physical beings that inhabit our universe include: 1-metre-tall mischievous green Goblins; 1.2-metre-tall lab-cloned

Greys; 2-metre-tall iridescent Grasshoppers; 2-metre-tall glowing Solars residing in suns; 2.5-metre-tall imperious Reptilians aka Lizards; 2-3-metre-tall contemplative Walking Plants; 3-metre-tall impassive Ants; 7-metre-tall cerebral Octopods; Integrators comprising organic and inorganic material; and intelligent Viruses.

The majority of those beings have moved beyond verbal language. They occasionally employ sounds, gestures, scents and colours but most communication is telepathic. Many of them are telekinetic. Some are adept at shapeshifting their physical bodies. Some are trans-dimensional (able to manifest in physical and other dimensions).

Let's shift the focus closer to home. The Milky Way galaxy.

* * *

The Milky Way is a barred spiral galaxy (a spiral galaxy with a central bar-shaped structure composed of stars). Ours is merely one of billions of galaxies in the observable universe. The stellar disk of the Milky Way galaxy is approximately 100,000 light years in diameter and about 1,000 light years thick. It is estimated to contain up to 400 billion stars. Sagittarius A* (pronounced Sagittarius A-star) is a supermassive black hole which marks the centre of the Milky Way. Most galaxies have a supermassive black hole at their centre. Your sun is approximately 30,000 light years from the centre of the Milky Way.

The beings that most interest us are humanoids. Humanoids have the same general structure, shape and height. One head, two arms, two legs, two forward-facing eyes. Humanoids are the most prevalent species in our galaxy.

After the Elohim had created physical life on stars and planets, they let Natural Law take its course. They kept a watchful eye on the protracted evolutionary process, noting with fascination the development of multifarious physical species. Eventually humanoid races began to emerge on a few planets. The Elohim chose to strategically enhance their DNA and observe the ramifications.

That intervention created rapidly advancing races in the Lyra and Boötes constellations of our galaxy, home of the Lyrans and Arcturians.

Lyra is a small constellation (star system or 'set of stars') which is visible in Earth's Northern Hemisphere from spring through autumn and in Earth's Southern Hemisphere during winter. Lyra is usually represented on star maps as an eagle carrying a lyre, and often referred to as Aquila Cadens ('eagle falling'). Vega, in the Lyra constellation, is the fifth brightest star in the night sky.

Over millennia the Lyrans developed into a highly advanced race who mastered genetics, technology, clean and free energy, propulsion systems, space travel, artificial intelligence (AI) and other scientific disciplines. Gradually they spread to other planets in the Lyra star system. Peace and harmony prevailed in their worlds.

Lyrans are 2.2-metre-tall humanoids, with lithe bodies, white skin, blonde or white hair, and blue eyes. They live in supreme physical health, their bodies designed to last 1,000 years. Other races often refer to them as the 'bird people'.

Every race becomes defined by a cultural signature. At heart, the Lyrans are scientists, explorers, experimenters and observers. They are characterised as academic, dispassionate, contemplative and tranquil.

Arcturus of the Boötes constellation is the brightest star in Earth's Northern Celestial Hemisphere and fourth brightest star in the night sky, after Sirius, Canopus and Alpha Centauri. Arcturus is about 180 times more luminous than your sun. All beings of this race are called Arcturians, after their sacred star; however, they inhabit many planets in their star system.

The principal planet is Mani, which means 'jewel', a glowing orb graced with tree-lined mountains, lush forests, sparkling rivers and gleaming oceans. The northernmost point of this planet hosts both the Pagoda, an enormous multi-tiered building housing the Planetary Government, and the crystal Temple of Arcturus, home of the Galactic Government. The highest level of the Galactic Government comprises ten Supreme Galactic Leaders, one secretive Time Lord, and a Light Seer linked to the Universal Council of Light.

Arcturus is exceptionally peaceful, free of even the slightest traces of poverty, crime and violence. Weapons are banned on all their planets and are only utilised by the Galactic Military to protect technologically weaker races from exploitation, enslavement or annihilation.

Arcturians are 1.8-metre-tall humanoids, with slender hairless bodies, greenish skin, and large black almond-shaped eyes. Three fingers on each hand is not a limitation as their advanced brains are naturally telekinetic and telepathic. Arcturian bodies have no sex organs; as such they use gender terms tentatively. Arcturians need only 3-4 hours rest in every 24 hour cycle. Their bodies last for approximately 500 years.

What is the cultural signature of the Arcturians? They are the leaders and protectors of the galaxy. Characterised as wise, virtuous and just. They prefer not to intervene in the internal affairs or evolution of other races. The motto 'Interference is Perilous' is their guiding light, a piece of wisdom accrued from millennia of experience.

Unfortunately, a third advanced race had developed in a distant galaxy. The 2.5-metre-tall humanoid Reptilians. Similar to the

Lyrans, they became master geneticists and space explorers. However, their cultural signature is aggressive domination. They are characterised as highly cognitive, deceptive, controlling and arrogant.

Long-lasting galactic wars erupted between the Lyrans and Reptilians. Two events shifted the security of our galaxy. The Arcturians, who steadfastly refused to engage in violence, had become the most technologically advanced beings in the Milky Way. Secondly, the Reptilians threatened the planet Mani. After the Cosmic War, and defeat of the Lizard beings, the Arcturians created the Galactic Federation to lead and protect the races of our galaxy.

The vast majority of star beings are benevolent and peaceable. Shared technology and united forces of the Galactic Federation inhibit the Reptilians and rogue star beings. The Federation also protects primitive planets and species.

With the Milky Way secure, the Lyrans focused on their aspirations: space exploration, colonisation and genetic experimentation. Genetic engineering, also called genetic modification, is the direct manipulation of an organism's genome (hereditary information encoded in DNA or RNA) using biotechnology. This mostly involves the insertion of new DNA into the host genome; it may also include the removal, addition or mutation of existing genes.

Many of our galaxy's humanoid races are the result of Lyran scientists experimenting with and upgrading indigenous inhabitants' DNA. Sirians, Orions, Pleiadeans, Earthlings (aka Terrans to star beings) are all descendants of the Lyran race.

And so the story moves to planet Earth.

* * *

The Lyrans had been watching Terra for a long time.

Planet Earth is 4.54 billion years old. Its history is measured broadly in Eons, which are divided into Eras, divided into Geologic Periods, and further divided into Epochs.

The Holocene is the geologic epoch that began in 9700 BC and continues to present day. It correlates with the current 'warm period' on Earth.

The Pleistocene is the geologic epoch from 2588000 to 9700 BC. It is colloquially referred to as the Ice Age as it incorporated the world's most recent period of repeated glaciations.

During the last glacial period, ice sheets reached their greatest extension approximately 24500 BC (known as the Last Glacial Maximum). An ice sheet is a mass of glacier ice covering a vast terrain.

Envisage the appearance of your planet by considering the following:

The Cordilleran Ice Sheet and Laurentide Ice Sheet covered most of Canada and a large portion of northern United States, as far south as present-day Washington state, Montana, Chicago, New York, New Hampshire and Nova Scotia.

The Patagonian Ice Sheet flowed south from present-day Puerto Montt, Chile, and Patagonia, Argentina, covering the south-western tip of South America.

The Weichselian Ice Sheet spread from the Scandinavian Mountains (present-day Norway and Sweden) as far south as Denmark and west to northern Russia.

The Antarctica and Greenland Ice Sheets.

Deglaciation of these ice sheets commenced in the Northern Hemisphere circa 17000 BC and in Antarctica circa 12500 BC, the latter precipitating a dramatic rise in sea level in 12500 BC.

A side note for ancient historians: The abrupt sea level rise in 12500 BC submerged most of the group of islands located in the South Pacific Ocean known as Lemuria. Lemurians are highly advanced trans-dimensional star beings from outside the Milky Way galaxy who settled on the islands near the Equator. The cultural signature of the Lemurians is seclusion, prayer, meditation, preternatural existence and deep connection to the Source. Those serene ethereal beings had fleeting interactions with the surrounding cultures, metaphysically influencing Japan, Southeast Asia, Australia, Hawaii and South America. After their islands were submerged they returned home. That, however, is a whole other story.

Similar to the Lemurians (who were the first star beings on your planet) the Lyrans scrutinised Earth for the optimal place to reside. The vast ice sheets north and south were counterpointed by temperate climates around the Equator and Tropic of Cancer. The monk-like Lemurians telepathically indicated their strong preference for seclusion and minimal contact. The Lyrans therefore chose to settle in the North Atlantic Ocean, on a huge island located near the Tropic of Cancer.

This would become known as Atlantis.

* * *

The Terran exploration crew comprised twelve Lyrans.

Cronus the leader (you remember him from another story). The males were Oceanus (sparks a memory), Hyperion, Iapetus, Koios and Krios; females were Rhea, Tethys (sparks a memory), Mnemosyne, Phoebe, Theia and Themis.

All were scientists. Their bodies contained the pure Lyran genetic code.

Lyrans communicate mostly via instant thought-force. Historically, as their telepathic abilities progressed, their ancient language faded. That beautiful language, also originally used by Arcturians, was known as Sanskrit. The Sanskrit alphabet consists of fifty letters, deemed as fifty sacred petals or sounds. Sanskrit is known as deva lingua or 'language of the gods'.

As your narrator, I am choosing to use Greek substitute names for the Lyran explorers. It will be easier to understand than Sanskrit. It may also help you interpret many of Earth's myths and mysteries.

The Lyrans had been watching Earth for some time.

The human ancestral family (aka great apes or hominids) had existed for millions of years, with the gradual speciation (splitting of lineages) of *Homo* the human from *Pan* the chimpanzee. *Homo sapiens* or anatomically modern humans only evolved about 200,000 years ago. Your scientists have actually discovered a modern human skeleton in Ethiopia dated to 193000 BC.

The unremitting evolution of both Earth and *Homo sapiens* made your planet suitable for a scientific expedition.

After an extensive reconnaissance, and consultation with the Lemurians, the Lyran scientists hovered their spaceship over a vast island near the Tropic of Cancer in the North Atlantic Ocean.

Viewed from high above, the large volcano (in the centre of the island) and smaller volcano (further to the south) created an impression of fiery eyes. For this reason, the Lyrans baptised their new home AlAtAkSI (Sanskrit, meaning 'having fiery eyes'). Over time, and repeated by discordant tongues, this became known as Atlantis.

Atlantis was termed an island because it was surrounded by water. Yet its dimensions made it bigger than many of your countries. The island was approximately 2,000 km north to south and 1,300 km east to west, totalling an area of circa 2.5 million square kilometres. Its northern tip aligned with the northern border of present-day Portugal; its southern tip aligned with the southern tip of present-day Florida. The island was positioned nearer Europe and Africa than North America.

To gain more perspective on its size, compare to present-day countries: Alaska is 1.72 million square kilometres; Mexico is 1.97 million square kilometres; Algeria is 2.38 million square kilometres; and India is 3.29 million square kilometres.

Atlantis was an extraordinarily beautiful island surrounded by a protective ring of mountains. The climate was lush and subtropical. Five rivers flowed in different directions from the centrally located dormant volcano to the ocean. A single river flowed from the smaller dormant volcano. The island was inhabited with elephants, monkeys and numerous animals. The rich soil produced verdant and abundant vegetation.

The Lyrans were delighted with their new home.

* * *

Atlantis was divided into ten geographic regions. Oceanus and Tethys had already requested dominion of the oceans. (Thousands of years later, humans would name the surrounding water 'Atlantic Ocean', an amalgam of Atlantis and Oceanus.) The remaining ten star beings chose a region and settled down.

Cronus and Rhea took the mid-eastern section next to the central volcano; a river flowed along each side of the territory. This was horizontally divided into two regions. Cronus presided over the larger upper section, which was designated as Greater Itza. Rhea presided over Lower Itza. Those regions derived their name from a contracted version of sarit kRtyA (Sanskrit, meaning 'ocean enchantment').

Oceanus and Tethys began to build an underwater domain. The land-based Lyrans commenced work on private residences. This was accomplished by utilising their advanced scientific knowledge and telekinetic abilities. They also had the assistance of the Hecatonchires, colossal AI (artificially intelligent) multi-limbed machines customarily stowed on the spaceship.

The Lyrans were first and foremost scientists. Although they overlaid their cultural and aesthetic preferences upon the island, they were not driven by ego or grandeur. They constructed exquisite homes in each region and a magnificent Crystal Temple in Greater Itza; however, the purpose was always based on functionality. The buildings were designed to integrate and harmonise with the natural environment. Consequently, the island was maintained in a state of pristine beauty.

Atlantis was a precarious and mysterious place, as the Lyrans soon learned. Although it was situated in a temperate zone in a desirable sector of the planet, and although it was strategically secure and suitably positioned for terrestrial expeditions, it concealed delicate flaws.

Firstly, its two dormant volcanos. To be clear about terminology, an active volcano (having had at least one eruption during the past 10,000 years) is either *erupting* or *dormant*. A dormant volcano is an active volcano that is not currently erupting, but may erupt again in the future. An *extinct* volcano has not erupted for at least 10,000 years and is not expected to erupt again in the future.

Secondly, the Mid-Atlantic Ridge (MAR) running beneath the island. The MAR is a mid-ocean ridge, a divergent tectonic plate boundary located along the floor of the Atlantic Ocean. In the

North Atlantic, it separates the North American and Eurasian Plates. The MAR rises 2-3 km above the ocean floor and has a rift valley at its crest marking the location at which the two plates are moving apart (caused by magma rising up the fractures and cooling on the ocean floor to form new ocean floor). The two plates are moving away from each other at an average spreading rate of 2.5 cm per year.

The Lyran scientists had been well trained in security, a legacy from bygone galactic wars. Hyperion assessed the volcanoes and reported a zero-threat prognosis. In fact, the huge centrally located volcano was largely hollow inside and descended to a great depth underground. Cronus capitalised on this opportunity. Using the Hecatonchires, he created within this dark abyss a storage facility for the Lyran spaceship. He named the volcano TrAtra (Sanskrit, 'defence'); discordant tongues gradually modified this to Tartarus.

When construction work in Atlantis was complete, the spaceship (with stowed Hecatonchires) was permanently parked in Tartarus. To further ensure security of their vital technology, Cronus created a ferocious energy field (known as the Elysian Field) in the throat of the volcano, behind which stood an AI humanoid-dragon called Campe who guarded the deep storage facility.

Five enormous saucer-shaped airships, also usually stowed within the spaceship, were left on land for local travelling and expeditions beyond Atlantis. The sixth airship was given to Oceanus and Tethys (the airships were fully operational underwater). These were silver-grey in colour, with a rapidly spinning outside, static centre, and advanced magnetic, anti-gravity and invisibility mechanisms. The airships were called Cyclops Ekam, Cyclops Dve, Cyclops Treeni, Cyclops Chatvaari, Cyclops Pancha and Cyclops Shat (Sanskrit, meaning 'one, two, three, four, five, six').

The magnificent Crystal Temple was built near the base of Tartarus in Greater Itza. This meant it lay within the domain of

Cronus and was centrally situated on the island. The temple was the nucleus of government, administration, technology and genetic research. The scientists regularly convened to discuss policy, strategy and implementation of their experiment on Earth.

The Lyrans were guided by strong ethics. In fact, Cronus personally embossed an inscription above the large stone archway leading into the Crystal Temple: Zakti dAyitva Azaya (Sanskrit, 'Power Responsibility Virtue'). It was a protocol heeded by these ancient star beings. They also abided by the Prime Directive to keep the Lyran genetic code pure. Lastly, the sacred numerals five and six were incorporated into their architecture, technology and spiritual life.

Walking through the stone archway was a humbling and perilous experience. It led directly into a spacious 10-metre-long tunnel embellished with scintillating engravings of trees. At the end a flurry of flaming swords swished dangerously. Behind this energy barrier an AI humanoid scanned energy signatures and demanded a password.

Once past that security feature, you entered a beautiful high-ceilinged room in which you were illumined with radiant energy to cleanse, disinfect and sterilise. This was a crucial process as the genetic laboratories were contained in the temple. Intriguingly, the following inscription was embossed above the entrance to the GenLabs: VRkSa JIvita (Sanskrit, 'Tree of Life').

The temple also housed the immense Crystal Room and Technology Rooms. Lyrans knew that light is the core of most advanced technologies. They used crystals to hold digital information (quantum bits stored and transmitted as pulses of light), for psychic and spiritual purposes (activating the third eye; surfing the multi-dimensions), for local and interstellar communication, for physical and mental healing, and for harnessing and distributing power.

On the roof of the temple, under a protective energy-dome, was the most important crystal of all. The six-sided Agni ZilA or 'Fire Stone'. This great crystal unceasingly absorbed the free energy of the cosmos. Cosmic energy is far beyond geothermal, solar, wind and wave energy. Airships, buildings, residences, vehicles, roads and devices were adorned with small crystals that induced power from the Fire Stone. Consequently, Atlantis later acquired the epithets Isle of Fire and Isle of Everlasting Light.

* * *

With the infrastructure in place, the Lyrans began surveying the landscape. Although the scientists already had food replicators in their private residences (which create meals and drinks directly from cosmic energy) they wished to ensure an abundance of food in the natural environment.

The subtropical climate and fertile volcanic soil had fostered the proliferation of wild orchards proffering delicious apples, pomegranates, grapes, pears, figs, avocados and olives. The towering central volcano was surrounded by extensive plains, which the scientists irrigated by creating a network of canals from nearby rivers. Vegetable gardens were laid out. Crops were planted.

The Lyrans travelled regularly to neighbouring continents, returning with a collection of seeds, bushes, trees and livestock from the (present-day) Mediterranean countries, Mexico, east coast of North America and northern parts of South America. The flora and fauna of Atlantis gradually became bountiful.

The star beings constantly augmented the GenLabs repository with recently obtained seeds and DNA samples. This crucial practice ensured the resources for genetic research, development and experimentation, a primary objective of the Lyrans.

It was now time to create a second generation of star beings to assist on Atlantis. Like most advanced races, Lyrans have spiritual-energetic sex for pleasure, deep connection and intimate consciousness-sharing. It is a beautiful, profound, ecstatic and loving experience. However, the creation of a new physical body is performed solely in a genetic laboratory. This guarantees the Prime Directive of maintaining pure Lyran genetic code; and it rules out genetic anomalies, disabilities and diseases.

A further ten Lyrans were created. They naturally grew into 2.2-metre-tall beings, with lithe bodies, white skin, blonde hair and blue eyes. They received a comprehensive education principally in the Crystal Temple. Humans would later refer to them as 'children of the gods'.

The next phase of the Atlantis experiment involved the importation of diverse humans from neighbouring continents. Naive immigrants were telepathically placated and given an orientation of their paradisiacal new home. They were allowed to roam freely on the island, but warned to stay away from the gods' private residences and the Crystal Temple.

The Lyran geneticists researched and experimented with human DNA then upgraded all humans on Atlantis. After removing defective and detrimental genes, a tiny snippet of DNA was inserted into every human genome. Once expressed (turned on) this snippet spawned additional folds or convolutions in the brain (a design which packs dense brain tissue into a small amount of space) and induced the neocortex to proliferate neurons. The unique intelligence of *Homo sapiens* stems from this modification and evolves as neural networks respond to stimulating challenges.

The first successfully altered male was named Adima (Sanskrit, 'first, aboriginal, primitive'); the first successfully altered female was named Hava (Sanskrit, 'alluring, dalliance').

The Lyrans were very clear about the division between 'us' and 'them'. Star beings were the rulers, creators, scientists and observers. Humans were created 'in their image' and encouraged to breed and enjoy paradise. Interaction between the creators and their creation was sporadic. All humans were taught to speak, read and write Sanskrit; in addition, they tutored basic skills like art and music. However, advanced knowledge was never shared.

Lyran 'gods' wore white robes with azure mantles. Humans roamed naked, naive and free. They were living in a land of plenty; there were no threats; and there was no need to work. Eventually the humans named their home UdyAna AiDa (Sanskrit, 'garden' 'containing everything that refreshes or strengthens'). Discordant ears beyond Atlantis later modified this to the 'Garden of Eden'.

Occasionally the scientists would return an altered human to its original country. This served two purposes. The evolutionary leap would spread slowly to the local population (through both genetics and communication). It also extended the dimensions of the anthropological experiment.

This is the reason your present-day archaeologists have discovered sophisticated cave paintings in: Chauvet cave in France, dated circa 30000 BC; Coliboaia cave in Romania, dated circa 30000 BC; El Castillo cave in Cantabria, Spain, dated circa 38000 BC; Pettakere cave on the island of Sulawesi in Indonesia, dated circa 38000 BC; and similar later paintings in Africa, Australia and South America. The petroglyphs (images created by removing part of a rock surface by incising, picking, carving or abrading) of Murujuga, aka Burrup Peninsula, in north-western Australia are also dated circa 38000 BC.

Although all the above primarily resulted from the Lyran experiment on your planet, there were, of course, subtle influences from the Lemurians.

* * *

While the land-based Lyrans were hard at work creating a paradise in Atlantis, Oceanus and Tethys were constructing a utopian underwater city entitled Avalina (Sanskrit, ava 'down from', lina 'hidden, concealed'). Over time, and repeated by discordant tongues, this became known as Avalon.

Inspired by the anthropological experiment, they also spent time in the GenLabs researching the physiology and genomes of disparate sea creatures. Their project took far longer and required input from other geneticists; however, ultimately a group of humans was altered to live comfortably on land and in water. Those beings, named Oceanids, inhabited the underwater city.

Oceanus and Tethys adored the ocean. After the successful adaptation of humans, they modified their own genomes too. This allowed them to reside permanently in the ocean and not depend on the technology of the airship. They also created their own children, whom they affectionately called 'water babies' and, as they grew older, 'nymphs'.

Oceanus became known as 'god of the oceans'. Nereids, nymphs of the seas, fell under his command. His appearance was imposing: a large figure attired in a silver robe, with full beard, and radiant white hair cascading over his shoulders. His voice was authoritative and powerful.

Tethys became known as the 'water-goddess'. Naiads, nymphs of fresh water, belonged to her domain. Her sensual silver-white body flowed through the streams, lakes and waterfalls, always swooshing toward the ocean. Her soft feminine voice swirled amid the aquatic consciousness. (Later she acquired the sobriquet Lady of the Lake.)

Oceanus was very fond of cetaceans – whales, dolphins and porpoises. He had utilised their DNA when creating the Oceanids. In gratitude, he inserted a tiny snippet of DNA into numerous cetacean genomes to produce increased brain convolutions and proliferation of intelligence-boosting spindle neurons. He loved the joyful kindness of dolphins and often used them as messengers between ocean and land.

Research and observation revealed intriguing facts about dolphins. When it is time to rest, these mammals hang motionless near the surface with the blowhole exposed, or swim slowly and surface occasionally for a breath, or rest on the floor in shallow water and surface intermittently for a breath. The reason for this behaviour is that dolphins have to be conscious to breathe ('voluntary breathers'). Therefore they cannot go into a complete sleep. Instead, dolphins employ unihemispheric slow-wave sleep, shutting down one hemisphere of the brain and closing the opposite eye, while the other half of the brain monitors the environment and controls breathing. Each half of the brain gets four hours of slow-wave sleep in every twenty-four hours.

The primary sense and communication of dolphins is auditory. Echo location and sonar messaging convey near-instant holographic images to aquatic companions, bypassing the need for an intermediate step (words, in the case of humans). Dolphins are also telepathic, which was the predominant connection among cetaceans, nymphs and Oceanids.

Tethys became enchanted by the genetically engineered unicorns or ekazRGga in Atlantis (Sanskrit, eka 'single', zRGga 'horn'). This beautiful creature appeared to be a small horse with pure white hair, blue eyes, cloven hooves and a long spiralled horn projecting from its forehead. After obtaining the genetic codes of the unicorn and dolphin she created a herd of silver-white water unicorns. These were named jala ekazRGga (Sanskrit, 'water unicorn') and they resided in Avalon.

The Lyrans were very pleased with their projects and experiments.

A phrase became common during this period.

'As above (Atlantis), so below (Avalon)'.

* * *

There are a few important things you should know about Lyrans.

Firstly, when a cohort of Lyran scientists arrives on a planet, they generally commit their lives to the research project. Hence, they stay with their genetic experiment and seldom return to their home world.

Secondly, although their physical bodies last about 1,000 years, these intriguing star beings can choose when to die and how to move forward. If they prefer not to transcend to a higher spiritual dimension upon death, they can simply transfer their consciousness to a newly created physical body. Thus they can choose an indefinite physical existence.

Thirdly, notwithstanding that it is regarded as unethical, upon physical death Lyrans can transfer their consciousness to another living being in close proximity. Upon entering this 'vehicle' they can repress the host's consciousness and take control of the body. Usually this is only a temporary measure enacted in an emergency. No harm is done to the host.

The Lyran cultural signature, as you recall, is defined as academic, dispassionate, contemplative and tranquil. This was reflected in the paradisiacal nature of their creations.

The star beings continued with exploration of your planet, regularly importing and upgrading multifarious humans (diverse races), as well as occasionally redepositing altered humans in their original habitats.

Many smaller islands dotted the waters to the east and west of Atlantis, all the way to the opposite continents. The 'children of the gods' created private residences on these islands and emulated the original project of their parents. In this way, the Lyrans had a widespread dominion.

Humans residing in Atlantis (and the other islands) learned Sanskrit, art, music and basic life skills. Oceanids also learned Sanskrit but seldom used it; they had been engineered for telepathic communication which was essential for underwater living.

The life span of altered humans ranged from 300-400 years. As the centuries passed and the population increased, the scientists chose overseers among the humans to manage their mundane affairs.

Under the leadership of Cronus and Rhea, a Golden Age lasting thousands of years existed in Atlantis and Avalon. The star beings' beneficence rippled across neighbouring countries too.

The 'gods' and upgraded humans lived peacefully and harmoniously in the 'Garden of Eden'. Humans were allowed to roam freely on the islands, but cautioned to keep away from the gods' private residences and the Crystal Temple. There was no need for laws or rules; everyone acted righteously. There was no need to work as they were surrounded by abundance. Disease and suffering did not exist in their world.

Life was good. Life was wonderful.

And then everything changed.

* * *

In 12500 BC deglaciation of the Antarctica ice sheet precipitated an abrupt dramatic rise in sea level. This submerged most of the group of islands located in the South Pacific Ocean known as Lemuria. Lemurians are highly advanced trans-dimensional star beings from outside the Milky Way galaxy who settled on the islands near the Equator circa 50000 BC. The cultural signature of the Lemurians is seclusion, prayer, meditation, preternatural existence and deep connection to the Source. After their islands were submerged they returned home.

However, that is not the entire story.

Around the same time as the deglaciation event, a Sirian spaceship entered into low Earth orbit (LEO is the first 160 to 320 km of space). Memories of previous distressing encounters with that intrusive race prompted the Lemurians' final decision to leave Earth.

Prior to their departure, those ethereal beings imparted a slice of wisdom, along with a warning about the Sirians, in a telepathic communiqué to Oceanus' cherished dolphins. The counsel was duly delivered to the Lyrans, who appreciated the information but dismissed the warning as trivial.

Ages ago the Lyrans had journeyed to the Sirian star system, conducted their customary research, and upgraded the indigenous inhabitants' genomes. The result was not as peaceable as Earth. The Sirians had voracious appetites and were soon clamouring for knowledge. They refused to wander blithely in a land of plenty.

The cohort of scientists eventually decided to share a portion of their advanced knowledge. However, it quickly became clear that the temperament of the Sirians was unsuited to this level of teaching. They lacked spiritual maturity, responsibility and virtue, traits that usually develop through extensive life experience. Protracted negotiations and discussions failed. The Lyrans chose to leave the star system and continue their work elsewhere in the galaxy.

Millennia had passed since that tumultuous event. The Sirians had made great progress, so Cronus was unconcerned by their presence. He placed the Cyclopes (plural of Cyclops) on high alert and waited for the aliens' arrival.

The unshielded Sirian spaceship landed in Greater Itza. The Lyrans welcomed them to planet Earth. A thought-provoking conference ensued. The Sirians expressed serious interest in the anthropological project. They agreed to settle on the northwest coast of Africa (present-day Morocco).

Ponder the motivations of advanced beings. What happens after disease, ageing, poverty, genetics and space travel have been conquered? What intrigues the various star races? How do their values coalesce with their activities? When do they transition to the status of creator?

The Lyrans were scientists and experimenters. They did not own your planet. Star beings were free to visit and stay on Earth. Hopefully they all interacted amicably.

The Sirians were the newcomers. They would be carefully monitored. Their involvement in the Atlantean project would be curtailed. Sharing of knowledge and technology would be limited.

Much would depend on how events unfolded.

A wait-and-see orientation was adopted.

* * *

The Sirians are very different to the Lyrans.

They are 2.1-metre-tall humanoids, with athletic bodies, dark reddish skin, auburn hair and green eyes. The pupils have vertical slits ('snake eyes') useful for predation and nocturnal hunting. Their bodies last about 800 years. Other races often refer to them as the 'snake people'.

The team that arrived on Earth comprised: Zeus (leader); males Poseidon, Dionysus, Apollo, Ares, Hephaestus and Hermes; females Hera, Demeter, Aphrodite, Artemis and Athena. The liaison officer and remote commander residing in the Sirian star system was Hades. (The gloom and murkiness of his home planet fostered the myth of the underworld.)

As your narrator, I am choosing to use Greek substitute names for the Sirians. It will be easier to understand than Sanskrit. It may also help you interpret many of Earth's myths and mysteries.

What is the cultural signature of the Sirians? They are hedonists, warriors and speculators. Characterised by strong emotions, impulsiveness, astuteness and loyalty.

Their initial interactions with the Lyrans were studiously planned. Sirians prefer intense and deep relationships. They knew their compatriots were dispassionate and academic. Hence, they treated the Lyran scientists with courtesy and respect. They visited Atlantis regularly and always adopted a sensitive and acquiescent demeanour.

As a gesture of goodwill, intermittent sharing of technology and knowledge took place. The Sirians worked hard to ingratiate themselves with the Lyrans. They gradually forged strong connections with the less experienced 'children of the gods'. When permitted, they walked among the humans and observed their lifestyle and customs.

For a long time, the star beings seemed to work well together.

One day a misguided 'child of the gods' disclosed details about the storage facility in Tartarus. This was a closely guarded secret among the Lyrans. The huge volcano concealed not only their principal technology but their primary means of interstellar travel. It was forbidden to share its existence and location.

Zeus was furious at the apparent deception and lack of trust. Instead of reacting, he buried the revelation and proceeded in the usual manner.

The Sirians had been brooding about another issue. The ethics of the anthropological experiment clashed with their values and ideology. Humans, though contented and carefree, were, from their perspective, no more than immature constrained monkeys in an exquisite zoo. These primitive beings should be evolved and liberated with higher knowledge.

There were many intense and heated discussions at the Atlantis conferences. The matter was never seriously progressed; instead, the Lyrans firmly vetoed all transition proposals.

Although the Sirians had grown closer to many 'children of the gods', they experienced the original Lyrans as supercilious and aloof. Not enough of their needs and values were being fulfilled.

Zeus could have ordered an exodus from the planet.

He could have left the Lyrans alone.

Instead, he contrived a strategy.

* * *

The Sirians had already developed a strong alliance with many 'children of the gods', both in Atlantis and Avalon. They persuaded them of the immorality of the anthropological experiment. They also created doubt about the level of sharing from their parents.

Zeus' crew were experts at stoking the flames of egocentricity and self-indulgence. In effect, they were spreading the ideology of hedonism. An uprising was gradually fermenting.

At the same time, they whispered subversive ideas as they walked and splashed among the Adimas, Havas and Oceanids in various locales. The snake people were sowing tempting ideas about the Tree of Knowledge.

It was time to put the final plan into action.

Zeus beguiled a wavering Lyran scientist to give him a tour of Tartarus. Once inside, he overpowered the guide and obtained the access codes. This gave him control over the ferocious energy field (known as the Elysian Field) in the throat of the volcano, as well as the AI humanoid-dragon who guarded the storage facility.

His crew were positioned nearby and promptly joined him at the Lyran spaceship. Although they were unable to activate the ship or Hecatonchires, they pillaged advanced technology. That is how Zeus acquired the Diamond Thunderbolt (Vajra) which became his personal weapon. Poseidon acquired a similar potent device called the Trident. The crew also stole invisibility helmets to secure a strategic advantage.

The ensuing 'war of the gods' was short-lived and decisive. The Lyrans could not utilise their defensive technology and resorted to battling with the Cyclopes. Explosions of light painted the tremoring skies. The concomitant loss of life included two original Lyrans (Hyperion and Koios) and over a dozen humans. It was a swift and triumphant coup d'état.

Once defeat was evident, Oceanus and Tethys escaped with a multitude of nymphs and dispersed into the oceans, seas and rivers. Poseidon, who seized power in Avalon, was unable to locate them.

Cronus, Rhea, Iapetus and Krios were incarcerated behind the energy field in Tartarus. Although they had access to their ship's amenities and food replicators, the main power crystal had been confiscated. Their prison was designated as Elysium due to the impenetrable Elysian Field.

Mnemosyne, Phoebe, Theia and Themis (remaining original female Lyrans) and the vacillating 'children of the gods' had no choice but to cooperate with the Sirians.

The Hecatonchires were removed to Greater Itza.

Zeus had magnificent plans.

* * *

The Sirians were predominantly hedonists and warriors.

Atlantis was divided among ten star beings, with Greater and Lower Itza naturally becoming the property of Zeus and Hera. Aphrodite declined to rule a region, instead opting to receive a lush island designated as Kypros. Poseidon inherited Avalon and a large island near present-day Bimini, which he renamed Poseidia. The various smaller islands were distributed among the gods.

Mnemosyne, Phoebe, Theia and Themis (remaining original female Lyrans) were allowed to stay in their residences in Atlantis. However, there was a price to be paid.

The Sirians adored the ostentatiousness and durability of noble metals. These metals, highly resistant to corrosion and oxidation, included gold, silver, platinum, tantalum and rhodium. Zeus commissioned Poseidon, Apollo, Ares and Hephaestus to survey the neighbouring countries for mining opportunities. In due course they enslaved various indigenous populations and transferred the Hecatonchires to expedite the project.

Mnemosyne and Themis were instructed to design a metal in the Sirians' favourite colour. After a few weeks of research and development, high-grade copper was blended with gold and platinum to produce a shimmering reddish metal called 'orichalcum'. The hedonistic star beings were gratified.

The Sirians understood the sacred numerals five and six, and were determined to incorporate these into the architecture and landscape of Atlantis.

Zeus built his abode on the highest point of the huge central volcano. This allowed him the tactical advantage of height, panoramic view and effortless monitoring of Tartarus and the Crystal Temple.

The rest of the Sirian gods built their mansions on plateaus lower on the mountain slopes. They regularly convened at Zeus' expansive premises to discuss matters pertaining to policy, government, administration and strategy for their adventure on Earth.

The gods' homes were resplendent. Stone walls inset with sheets of orichalcum; statues of adolescents holding crystalline torches; courtyards decorated with mosaics of gemstones; fountains spewing fresh water; huge sculpted wooden doorways; statues of animals in gold and silver; lavish banquet halls with regal chairs; spacious rooms embellished in gold and orichalcum; and walls adorned with exquisite art and woven hangings.

After they constructed their glorious mansions on the mountain, each god erected a colossal self-statue in their individual region of Atlantis. Aphrodite and Poseidon, who did not govern in Atlantis, built self-statues on their private islands.

Zeus decided to build an extra layer of security around the Crystal Temple in Greater Itza. Adhering to the sacred numerals, the temple was surrounded by five sculpted concentric rings of water and land. The innermost islet, bearing the temple, was encircled with a high wall inset with orichalcum, followed by a 500-metre-wide moat. Then a 1,000-metre-wide ring of land, a high wall inset with silver, and another 500-metre-wide moat. Finally, a 1,000-metre-wide ring of land, a high wall inset with gold, and a 500-metre-wide moat. Once complete, the venerated temple was renamed Temple of Zeus.

Keeping with his enterprising vision, the river (northern boundary of Itza) was widened and deepened, then channelled into a broad canal which traversed the concentric rings. This would allow ships to sail from the water moats, along the river and into the ocean.

Zeus' colossal self-statue was positioned 500 metres beyond the outermost concentric ring, its back toward the temple and Mount Tartarus, and gazing eastward at the present-day Strait of Gibraltar (entry point into the Mediterranean Sea from the Atlantic Ocean).

Poseidon, who ruled a large island near present-day Bimini, was inspired by the vision of Zeus. He proceeded to construct a lavish Temple of Poseidon and surrounded it with identical concentric rings, traversed by a 9,300-metre-long canal that accessed the ocean. Whereas Atlantis was bordered by a ring of protective mountains, Poseidon built a huge wall inset with platinum to border his entire island. Poseidia became known as the gleaming jewel of the ocean.

The Temple of Poseidon was overlaid with gold and silver on the outside; its huge sculpted wooden doorways gave ingress to enormous rooms girdled by orichalcum-covered walls, floors and pillars; life-size golden statues of the Sirian gods preceded the colossal statue of Poseidon, displayed standing in a chariot drawn by six winged horses, and accompanied by thirty ocean nymphs riding dolphins.

The Sirian star beings transformed the Atlantean Empire (Atlantis and surrounding islands) into a scintillating opulent paradise. Awe-inspiring architecture and sumptuousness merged with gurgling rivers, tranquil lakes, flowing canals, lush vegetation, cultivated orchards and prolific crops. It was a magnificent and delightful Garden of Eden.

* * *

You will recall that the Lyrans wore white robes with azure mantles. The Sirians preferred to dress in loose-fitting red trousers with red-and-white tunics. Humans roamed naked, naive and free.

The new rulers, also known as the 'snake gods', awakened the Tree of Knowledge in the Temple of Zeus (previously the Crystal Temple). A common present-day misconception is that the Tree of Knowledge elucidated 'good and evil'. In truth, this powerful crystalline interface taught 'knowledge of everything'.

The exception was information pertaining to the Tree of Life, which was kept secret. This referred to genetics, genetic engineering, cell regeneration and repair, and indefinite physical existence.

The Sirians taught the humans about textile fibres, weaving, dyes and pigments, and how to manufacture clothing and beautify the body; about noble metals, base metals and gemstones, and how to transmute these into jewellery, art, ornaments, furniture and weapons; about plants, herbs, tinctures and alcohol, and how to access different states of consciousness; about mathematics, physics, astronomy, meteorology and geology, and how to predict future events on Earth.

Humans had been designed with high intelligence and made rapid progress in their learning. As with all humanoid 'children', they were also assimilating attitudes, beliefs and behaviours from observing their new role models.

Therein resided the flaw in the plan.

The Lyran scientists may have appeared aloof and dispassionate, but they demonstrated exemplary ethics. They adhered to the protocol of 'Power Responsibility Virtue' and followed the Prime Directive to keep the Lyran genetic code pure. They were remote observers of the anthropological experiment and maintained sporadic interaction with humans.

The Sirians were hedonists driven by strong emotions and impulsiveness. They had no qualms about having sexual intercourse with whomever they desired.

Zeus mated with the (unwilling) Lyran females Mnemosyne and Themis. The Sirian gods mated with each other, though their strong appetites eroded fidelity. Over time, those licentious star beings had sexual intercourse with Lyran 'children of the gods', nymphs, humans and the occasional animal.

The Sirians' reckless and unconstrained sexual activity resulted in a diversity of weird and wonderful creatures wandering the Atlantean Empire.

Mating with 'children of the gods' and nymphs produced exotic beings with peculiar characteristics, ranging from alluring and powerful to monstrous and malicious. Mating with humans produced 3-metre-tall giants (known as demi-gods) who were strong, resourceful, intelligent and lived for hundreds of years. Mating with animals produced fantastic and bizarre therianthropes

(Greek, therion 'wild animal', anthropos 'human') like satyrs, centaurs, harpies and drakainas.

The inundation of strange and monstrous creatures decreased the peace and security in Atlantis and Avalon. Gangs of humans, often accompanied by a demi-god, tracked and hunted dangerous beasts. There were many human casualties and fear steadily seeped into anthropological consciousness.

The Sirian regime was engendering a radical change in Atlantean culture and lifestyle.

* * *

Under the leadership of Cronus and the Lyrans, a Golden Age lasting thousands of years existed in Atlantis and Avalon. The gods and upgraded humans lived peacefully and harmoniously.

Under the leadership of Zeus and the Sirians, a Silver Age lasting only 1,700 years existed in Atlantis and Avalon. It was characterised by strife, struggle, conflict and chaos.

Over the centuries under Sirian rule, humans were taught the art of making weapons, armour and war. A huge fleet comprising cargo vessels and warships was built. The navy was docked in Atlantis and Poseidia. Soldiers were positioned in watchtowers along the primary rivers and canals. Guards were deployed on the walls surrounding the Temple of Zeus and Temple of Poseidon. Upgraded humans were mentored to become leaders. Eventually they were commanding ships to neighbouring countries, transporting precious cargo, managing mining operations and oppressing primitive humans.

Zeus systematically extended the reach and sovereignty of the Atlantean Empire into the Americas, North Africa and Mediterranean countries.

Atlantis was renowned for its lush natural resources, advanced agriculture, grandiose construction, pioneering metallurgy, sophisticated engineering and seagoing navigation. The burgeoning population and surplus of food allowed for division of labour and specialised jobs, ranging from artisans and artists to sailors and shipwrights.

During the Silver Age, most of the Atlantean humans became promiscuous, greedy and egotistic. Although they lived in a land of plenty, they were seldom satisfied. They saw the opulence of the Sirians and desired lavish residences and possessions. Fashion became important with concomitant clothing, makeup and jewellery. There were few ethical guidelines and positive role models. Outbursts of violence occurred regularly.

Certain sectors strove to increase scientific knowledge and were taught by the Sirians. Over time, they too were discontented. Progress was slow. Humans clamoured for advanced knowledge and access to the Tree of Life. (In Tartarus, Cronus was reminiscing about the Lyran research expedition to the Sirian star system, and musing on 'karma' and the 'cycle of life'.)

The Adimas, Havas and Oceanids remembered that two original Lyrans had been killed in the 'war of the gods'. They had learned that their gods were mortal. The subsequent teachings and behaviour of the Sirians were the final blow to the pedestal. Evidently, all that separated the star beings and humans was knowledge and technology.

The Sirians had little interest in genetic experimentation. They did, however, continue the Lyran practice of importing diverse humans from neighbouring continents. Unfortunately, Atlantean humans bred with the 'fresh stock', which gradually diluted their divine genetic code. The life span of many humans decreased to less than 100 years.

A small devoted sect offered a glimmer of hope. Choosing to wear white robes with azure mantles, and abiding by the protocol of

'Power Responsibility Virtue', these upgraded humans followed the 'old ways'. The group called themselves the Holy Order of Cronus (disguised as the acronym 'Horus' to avoid scrutiny from the Sirians). A design of a falcon was sewed inside the left sleeve of their robes to symbolise allegiance to the 'bird god'.

Phoebe and Theia (untouched original female Lyrans) and four unwavering Lyran 'children of the gods' devoted themselves to this company of humans. The sect lived simply and righteously, eschewing promiscuity, greed, egotism, anger and violence. The Lyrans shared confidential and advanced knowledge with them, each member sworn to an oath of secrecy.

In gratitude for mating with the (unwilling) Lyran females Mnemosyne and Themis, Zeus promised to protect from harm all those associated with the peaceable, devout Horus sect.

While the members of the sect regularly brought offerings of fruit and flowers to the Lyran gods, the majority of Atlantean humans grew conceited and disrespectful to the Sirians. These petulant spoiled 'adolescents' refused to heed the instructions of their leaders. Reverence and courteousness ceased.

This rebellious behaviour angered Zeus. It also contravened an important value in Sirian culture: loyalty.

There was trouble in paradise.

* * *

Zeus sat in his lavish mountain residence, gazing upon the verdant scenery of Atlantis. Although he was a man of his word (loyalty being a crucial value), he was not a patient or calm being. He took what he wanted and did as he pleased.

They had arrived on Earth in 12500 BC. Spent centuries investing knowledge in these ungrateful humans. Yet they were never satisfied. They clearly had reached a point where they wanted to become like the gods. All they needed was access to crystal technology and the Tree of Life.

Admittedly it was his fault that the Atlantean Empire was overrun with giants, monsters, savage animals and grotesque creatures. Pure-bred Atlantean humans were tall, slender and highly intelligent, with skin of varying colour (originating from different continents) and blue eyes (resulting from insertion of Lyran DNA). Hair colour ranged from blonde to ebony. These days he seldom saw blue eyes. Many humans appeared sickly. Red hair predominated.

It was now 10800 BC. Everyone seemed angry. Except those pathetic followers of Horus, or whatever they were called. At least they knew how to behave themselves. They were never impertinent or insolent.

Perhaps this chaos is why the Lyrans had left his star system ages ago.

Fury welled up in him. It was time to clear this mess and expunge the mistakes.

He grabbed the data crystal and beckoned his Sirian compatriots. They sat down in the large viewing room. Scrolling back in time, Zeus found the extinction event and opened it.

As your narrator, I am, as usual, using Earth terms and references in order to provide clarity.

From the Sirians' perspective, the last extinction event on your planet occurred around 65 million years ago. The Cretaceous-Paleogene (K-Pg) or Cretaceous-Tertiary (K-T) was a mass extinction event that wiped out 80% of the plant and animal species on Earth (including the dinosaurs).

A gigantic comet hurtled into your planet at Chicxulub on Mexico's Yucatan Peninsula. The collision released thousands of times the energy of all the nuclear bombs on present-day Earth. It immediately generated earthquakes, tsunamis, and global firestorms sparked by an intense heat pulse. It also created an 'impact winter', resulting from the enormous amount of dust, ash and sulfuric acid that ejected into the global atmosphere and blocked out the sun. Rain and ocean water became acidic. The dark winter lasted more than twenty years. The entire planet was affected simultaneously.

The Sirians knew that comets travel much faster than asteroids, with consequent devastating kinetic energy.

Zeus explained that he wanted to wipe out the sullied anthropological experiment in much the same way. A heated discussion ensued. The female gods Demeter, Aphrodite and Artemis pleaded for a compassionate approach. His decision was swift and final.

Ares and Hephaestus were ordered to take the Sirian spaceship, locate a suitable comet and redirect it to the Atlantean Empire.

Atlantis was going to be destroyed.

* * *

Demeter notified the Lyran females of the impending cataclysm. She returned the spaceship's main power crystal with the assurance that the Tartarus access codes would follow soon. The codes were required to deactivate the energy field in the volcano and liberate Cronus, Rhea, Iapetus and Krios.

Zeus controlled the fleet of Cyclopes. With the assistance of Mnemosyne and Themis, more of those craft had been produced over the centuries. The blueprint and build technology lay in the Temple of Zeus. Those two Lyran females had right of entry into the temple because of their apparent loyalty and shared children.

Stealthily and slowly, they copied all the sacred information onto the twelve Knowledge Stones (aka data crystals). As scientists they knew it was imperative to securely store research data.

You will recall that Lyrans used crystals to hold digital information (quantum bits stored and transmitted as pulses of light), for psychic and spiritual purposes (activating the third eye; surfing the multi-dimensions), for local and interstellar communication, for physical and mental healing, and for harnessing and distributing power.

To be clear about terminology, a 'stone' (aka gem, gemstone, jewel, precious stone or semi-precious stone) is a piece of mineral crystal in cut and polished form.

The six-sided Agni ZilA or 'Fire Stone' (aka power crystal) unceasingly absorbed the free energy of the cosmos (when uncovered). Airships, buildings, residences, vehicles, roads and devices were adorned with small crystals that induced power from the Fire Stone. In the beginning, there was one Fire Stone on top of the Crystal Temple in Atlantis. Later, ten Fire Stones were situated across the Atlantean Empire (including one in Avalon); the remaining two were locked in the Temple of Zeus. Fire Stones are large transparent white crystals that glow with a golden light when charged with cosmic energy.

The SaMvAda ZilA or 'Communication Stone' (aka transceiver crystal) is a rose-pink, light-crimson crystal used for local and interstellar communication. There were ten Communication Stones utilised across the Atlantean Empire (including one in Avalon); the remaining two were locked in the Temple of Zeus.

The VijJAna ZilA or 'Knowledge Stone' (aka data crystal) is an emerald-green crystal used to hold digital information. These twelve stones were stored securely in the Temple of Zeus.

The JIvita ZilA or 'Healing Stone' (aka life-force crystal) is an azure crystal which radiates potent energy that dispels pathogens. It is also wielded for cell regeneration and repair, and physical and mental healing. These twelve stones were kept in the Temple of Zeus.

The AdhyAtmika ZilA or 'Spirit Stone' (aka transcendence crystal) is a mauve crystal utilised for psychic and spiritual purposes (activating the third eye; surfing the multi-dimensions). These twelve stones were cached in the Temple of Zeus.

Covertly briefed by Mnemosyne and Themis, Phoebe and Theia convened a meeting of the Horus sect on a small uninhabited island east of Atlantis. They warned the humans of the disaster initiated by the Sirians and instructed them to surreptitiously build a Cyclops. They were supplied with the blueprint and building technology. A huge energy field, resonating beyond Sirian perception, camouflaged their activities.

Over the next few weeks, Mnemosyne and Themis smuggled genetic data, seeds and DNA (representing nearly all human, animal and plant life) from the Temple GenLabs onto the small island, and finally onto the Horus airship.

As the Cyclops neared completion, the Lyran females brought one of each of the five sacred stones (Fire, Communication, Knowledge, Healing, Spirit) and stowed them in the enormous saucer-shaped airship. (The term 'airship' is a misnomer, of course, as this vehicle was fully operational on and under water.)

The newly built airship was baptised NaukA (Sanskrit, 'boat, ship, ark'). Discordant ears beyond Atlantis later modified this to 'Noah Ark'. The advanced humans, collectively known as Manu

Vaivasvata (Sanskrit, manu 'intelligent human', asvata 'unselfishness, having no property'), boarded the vessel and waited for signs from the heavens.

* * *

The year was 10800 BC.

A huge comet was hurtling toward planet Earth.

This is the part where you need to pay close attention.

As a reminder, planet Earth is 4.54 billion years old. Its history is measured broadly in Eons, which are divided into Eras, divided into Geologic Periods, and further divided into Epochs.

The Holocene is the geologic epoch that began in 9700 BC and continues to present day. It correlates with the current 'warm period' on Earth.

The Pleistocene is the geologic epoch from 2588000 to 9700 BC. It is colloquially referred to as the Ice Age as it incorporated the world's most recent period of repeated glaciations.

During the last glacial period, ice sheets reached their greatest extension approximately 24500 BC (known as the Last Glacial Maximum). An ice sheet is a mass of glacier ice covering a vast terrain.

Envisage the appearance of your planet by considering the following:

The Cordilleran Ice Sheet and Laurentide Ice Sheet covered most of Canada and a large portion of northern United States, as far south as present-day Washington state, Montana, Chicago, New York, New Hampshire and Nova Scotia.

The Patagonian Ice Sheet flowed south from present-day Puerto Montt, Chile, and Patagonia, Argentina, covering the south-western tip of South America.

The Weichselian Ice Sheet spread from the Scandinavian Mountains (present-day Norway and Sweden) as far south as Denmark and west to northern Russia.

The Antarctica and Greenland Ice Sheets.

The Younger Dryas is a geologic period from 10800 to 9700 BC. The Earth had been gradually warming since the Last Glacial Maximum in 24500 BC. From 10800 BC there was a sudden decline in temperature (2-6 degrees Celsius) over most of the Northern Hemisphere. This cooler period continued until the planet started warming in 9700 BC which marked the beginning of the Holocene epoch.

What caused the anomalous Younger Dryas cooling period?

The answer is the comet directed by the Sirians.

A gigantic comet moving in a south-easterly direction (known to present-day scientists as the Clovis Comet or Younger Dryas Comet) entered Earth's atmosphere somewhere over Canada then broke into multiple fragments. Although some exploded in the air, most of the enormous fragments collided with the Cordilleran and Laurentide ice sheets. Many fragments streaked across the Atlantic Ocean, impacting the Atlantean Empire and the Weichselian ice sheet. A few darted across the Mediterranean Sea, striking into Turkey, Syria and Lebanon.

The colossal explosive energy and heat from multiple impacts into the Cordilleran and Laurentide ice sheets caused an extensive cataclysmic meltdown. The resultant immense flood destroyed all flora and fauna in its path, finally entering the ocean and creating a dramatic rise in sea level.

The massive rush of fresh water also negatively affected the Atlantic Meridional Overturning Circulation which is an important component of Earth's climate system. AMOC refers to the northward flow of warm water in the upper layers of the Atlantic and the southward flow of cold water in the deep Atlantic. This ocean circulation system conveys a substantial amount of heat from the Tropics and Southern Hemisphere toward the North Atlantic, where the heat is dispersed into the atmosphere. The disruption of the AMOC caused a decline in temperature in the Northern Hemisphere.

As with the dinosaur-annihilating comet 65 million years ago, the multiple explosions of the Younger Dryas Comet in 10800 BC released thousands of times the energy of all the nuclear bombs on present-day Earth. Devastating high-temperature shock waves were followed by tornado-like winds, earthquakes, tsunamis and global firestorms.

The colossal impacts ejected dust, ash, soot and smoke into the global atmosphere which blocked out the sun and caused an 'impact winter' for over twenty years. Your planet moved into the global cooling period that geologists designate as the Younger Dryas.

The Younger Dryas Comet cataclysm explains the myths and stories conveyed by numerous Northern Hemisphere cultures and religious historical texts. Excerpts include: 'sky serpent (Sirian comet) creating a huge windstorm and destroying all living creatures'; 'fierce rain of celestial fire'; 'sent down ferocious thunderbolts to wage a great battle against humans and giant animals'; 'assault of the celestial snake (Sirian comet) called the Great Leaping One that pierces the Earth'; 'dropped the sky one day, causing the Earth to be consumed in flames, then deluged by a great flood'; 'humans were destroyed by lightning from the sky and rain, and all the land was submerged in water'; 'flood with black rain, hail, mist and freezing cold'; 'rain fell upon the earth for forty days and forty nights'; 'flood water surged upon the land one hundred and fifty days'; 'the Earth was inundated by a great flood and plunged into darkness by the disappearance of the sun'; 'the faces of the sun and moon were covered'; 'cloudy and twilight all over the world'; 'warning of fatal winters bringing fierce treacherous frost'; 'wiped out every living thing that was upon the face of the land, from humans to animals to creeping things to birds'.

A side note for the scientifically-minded: 'Cosmic impact markers' include nanodiamonds (microscopic diamonds formed under rare conditions of tremendous shock, pressure and heat), high-temperature melt-glass, carbon spherules, metallic microspherules and iridium. Present-day scientists know of only two layers of sediment distributed across several continents that display an assembly of cosmic impact markers. Those layers are situated at the Younger Dryas boundary 10800 BC and the Cretaceous-Tertiary boundary 65 million years ago.

Planet Earth has been devastated by two comets.

* * *

The advanced humans waited inside the newly built Cyclops (designated as NaukA) for signs from the heavens. Phoebe and Theia (mentors of the Horus sect) had instructed them not to activate the airship until the Sirians had left the planet. They had to avoid detection by Zeus.

Demeter delivered the Tartarus access codes to Mnemosyne and Themis, who immediately liberated Cronus, Rhea, Iapetus and Krios. The Hecatonchires and five original Cyclopes were hastily transferred onto the spaceship (one original Cyclops had been destroyed in the 'war of the gods'). Cronus demanded the return of the sacred crystals; Zeus raised his hands in mock surrender. The Lyrans accessed the temple and retrieved all the crystals; then hurriedly collected the dispersed Fire and Communication Stones. When they collected the Fire Stones all the islands lost power.

The Sirians retained absolute control. They waited until the Lyrans had left the Earth before completing their final tasks. As comet fragments began to streak across the Atlantic Ocean, Zeus initiated their exodus. The Sirian spaceship lingered in low Earth orbit for a long while, observing the destruction of human and animal life.

NaukA was unable to activate in time. Fortunately, it was parked on an island east of Atlantis, furthest away from the brunt of the cataclysm. The energy shield offered complete protection, but as long as Zeus watched from high above, the airship had to remain in position. Soon the flood arrived and the vessel was buoyed and carried away by the rising water.

Outside was a frightening scene. Ceaseless black rain for six weeks. Ferocious ocean waves and endless darkness. Inside the ark, the Fire Stone provided power and light, and food replicators kept them nourished. However, their home was gone. The star beings had departed. Earth was being ravaged.

After five harrowing months NaukA came to rest on a mountain in the eastern extremity of present-day Turkey. The Manus stayed in the vessel and waited for the flood waters to subside. Land slowly appeared over the next few months. Birds were released but they always returned to the ark.

A year had passed since the initial cosmic onslaught. One day a luminous hummingbird with green, silver and gold plumage flitted into NaukA. It carried in its beak an olive leaf, representing the survival and fertility of local plant life.

Mysteriously, at the same moment, the Communication Stone lit up with a message: 'Go out of the ark, all of you. Use the seeds to rebuild and replenish life. Be fruitful and multiply on the Earth.'

The advanced humans flew the airship to low ground, landing in present-day Göbekli Tepe near the southern border of Turkey. They debarked and surveyed the primitive wilderness. Gradually they began to encounter clans of hunter-gatherers. Soon the realisation dawned. They were now the gods. It was crucial to adhere to the protocol of 'Power Responsibility Virtue'. They vowed to carry out the vision of their mentors.

The Manus knew they had to rebuild and replenish the Earth. They had the technology and knowledge to effectuate this mission. Emancipated from Sirian tyranny, they chose to emblazon a design of a falcon on the front of their robes. The Manus became known as the followers of Horus.

Over the ensuing decades the followers of Horus travelled across the present-day Middle East. They built immense structures in reverence to the Lyrans; taught basic mathematics, physics, astronomy, meteorology, geology and agriculture; and instilled the values of tolerance, respect, compassion and kindness.

In a sense, the Manus were striving to recreate Atlantis. Bear in mind that Earth had recently experienced its second extinction-level event. A huge swathe of human and animal life had been destroyed. The remaining humans were scattered in areas where the cataclysm had not reached. Those hunter-gatherers were relatively primitive in evolutionary terms.

The Manus appeared as gods to the nomadic tribes. The leader of the advanced humans was named Adhipa (Sanskrit, 'commander, regent'), later translated as Uanna (Babylonian) then Oannes (Greek). Adhipa had a crew of eleven Manus, comprising the Seven Sages (including him) and Five Builders.

The Sages were experts in academic subjects and the Builders were masters of architecture, engineering and construction.

Interestingly, present-day historians regard 'Ad' as one of the original Arab tribes. The tribe's members were called 'Adites' aka 'sons of the fire mist'. The Adites are remembered by the Arabs as sophisticated architects and builders.

Having landed near the border of southern Turkey, they travelled through Mesopotamia. Mesopotamia (Ancient Greek, 'land between rivers') originally Mijagetq (Ancient Armenian, 'land between rivers') refers to the area of the Tigris-Euphrates river system, which corresponds roughly to most of present-day Iraq, plus Kuwait, the eastern parts of Syria and south-eastern Turkey. Considered by your archaeologists to be one of the cradles of civilisation, Mesopotamia later included Sumer and the Akkadian, Assyrian and Babylonian empires.

The preceding details elucidate the Mesopotamian myth of the Seven Apkallu (Akkadian, 'sages') who brought mathematics, architecture, construction, laws, crafts and agriculture to the land. They were said to have lived 'before the flood' and frequently portrayed as fish-men or bird-men in Mesopotamian art and sculpture (symbolising 'emerging from the ocean' and 'flying in the air'). The sages were also depicted as bearded men holding a bag, representing the sowing of seeds (knowledge and agriculture). They were often considered as 'sorcerers' or 'magicians' by primitive tribes.

Similar myths are found in ancient Egypt and India. Both mention a calamitous flood and Seven Sages (Egypt) or Seven Rishis (India) who are bringers of the gifts of civilisation, builders of magnificent temples and teachers of advanced knowledge.

That piece of ancient history also explains the Neolithic Revolution (aka Agricultural Revolution) which was the transition of numerous human cultures from a lifestyle of nomadic hunter-gathering to one of agriculture and settlement. The Neolithic Revolution commenced in the Middle East and Asia circa 10700 BC. Agriculture and settlement fostered population growth, surplus food production, division of labour, trade and related technology.

Your present-day archaeologists are rediscovering the work of the Manus (aka followers of Horus or Apkallus):

Many of these ancient structures are linked to astronomy, with distinct solar, lunar and stellar alignments. The builders manifested advanced knowledge of surveying, architecture, engineering and construction.

Göbekli Tepe (Turkish, 'Navel Hill'), originally known as Portasar (Armenian, 'Navel Hill'), is an archaeological site atop a mountain ridge in south-eastern Turkey. The tell (a mound formed by the accumulated remains of ancient settlements) comprises circles of massive stone pillars, each weighing up to 20 tons. Your archaeologists assert these are the world's oldest known megaliths, dated circa 10700 BC.

Baalbek is an archaeological site in Lebanon. This ancient complex was constructed with enormous megalithic blocks, each weighing from 100 to 1,500 tons. Typical precision-engineering was employed by the builders. Baalbek megalithic site is contemporaneous with the megalithic site of Göbekli Tepe.

The Great Sphinx of Giza was built circa 10500 BC and was originally entirely a lion (had a lion's head). Your archaeologists affirm that ancient Egyptians associated Horus with the Great Sphinx. The pyramids were constructed thousands of years later.

In India your archaeologists have uncovered a huge man-made structure in Poompuhar, Tamil Nadu dated circa 10300 BC.

The followers of Horus did not possess the entire knowledge and wisdom of the Lyrans; however, they gradually created evolutionary ripples in the sparse hunter-gatherer populations. It was a relatively slow process as they tried to recreate the vision of their gods.

Atlantis was fading to a distant memory. A paradise lost to the depravity of the Sirians.

Little did they know the star beings would return.

* * *

The decisive moment was when the Manus tried to build a city to emulate Atlantis.

After numerous journeys into Egypt and India, they decided to create a paradisiacal city on a fertile plain between the Tigris and Euphrates rivers. The landscape reminded them of their lost home. The location was also appropriately positioned as a central base for their activities.

The newly educated humans worked alongside the 'builder gods' to construct a sprawling metropolis and a huge tower to support the Fire Stone. They named the city DvAra AreNu (Sanskrit, 'Gate of Gods') known in the future as Babel (Akkadian, 'Gate of God').

This was the first time the Manus had removed a sacred Stone from NaukA. No longer shielded by the ark, the large white crystal glowed as it absorbed the energy of the cosmos. Its unique energy signature naturally rippled into the atmosphere.

Cronus was elated and concerned when the distinctive energy was detected. The Lyrans had stayed away from Earth to avoid drawing attention to the followers of Horus. There was always the possibility that the impulsive Sirians were monitoring the planet.

The Lyrans took that course of action despite the formidable intervention by the Arcturians.

The Arcturians, you will recall, are the leaders and protectors of the galaxy. They prefer not to intervene in the internal affairs or evolution of other races. The motto 'Interference is Perilous' is their guiding light, a piece of wisdom accrued from millennia of experience.

Although the Arcturians had ignored the initial skirmish between the Lyrans and Sirians, the comet cataclysm had blipped on their ethical radar. A firm warning had been issued and the Sirians were forbidden from returning to Earth. The decades following the cataclysm had swathed Zeus in regret. The Council of Sirians had subsequently vowed never to destroy a humanoid race again (unless it was an act of war).

And so, five hundred years after leaving your planet, the Lyrans returned.

The enormous spaceship hovered over the tower and scanned the expansive city. Soon the Cyclops was located and nearby a few white-robed beings. They recognised the falcon insignia ... followers of Horus!

Cronus was engulfed with disparate sentiments. Relieved that the Atlanteans had survived the deluge. Pleased to witness the rebuilding and replenishing of Earth. Assuaged of some of his guilt over deserting Atlantis. However, the Manus were overstepping the bounds. Sharing technology and advanced knowledge with a primitive civilisation always led to disaster. It was imperative that a certain level of emotional and spiritual maturity first be reached.

The Sirians and the Atlantean Empire were exemplars of that truth.

Cronus retrieved the Fire Stone then blasted the tower to smithereens. The Manus were angry and confused as the spaceship descended. They waited anxiously to meet their gods.

The Lyrans approached with affable smiles and open arms. They commended the Manus for their survival and progress on Earth. They explained the need to curtail the teachings. Evolution had to take its natural course with only minimal and strategic intervention.

Five hundred years was a long time to be free of their gods. The Manus had learned the joy of independence and self-responsibility. They were now visionaries and creators. They had learned from observing the mistakes of the Sirians. A cautious and edifying blueprint was being instituted in Mesopotamia.

Cronus described how they had surveyed the Atlantic Ocean and found Atlantis and many of the islands intact. They were going to reclaim and restore the Atlantean Empire. He offered the Manus the opportunity to return to Atlantis and become leaders of a new human race. He informed them of the Sirian vow never to destroy a humanoid race again.

The followers of Horus respectfully declined. They preferred ideological freedom, self-determination and security.

The Lyrans respected their viewpoint. However, to maintain the natural evolutionary process, Cronus confiscated the Cyclops and remaining sacred Stones. The Manus might retain higher knowledge but they were certainly not going to share advanced technology.

Leaving Adhipa in DvAra AreNu, he forced the rest of the Manus onto the spaceship. Then he deposited each of the remaining eleven in a different country. This effectively isolated the Apkallu and slowed the dissemination of teachings.

The frustrated Manus found themselves amid foreign tongues. Communication would not be possible until they had mastered the local language. It would take many years before they could share basic academic concepts with the primitive hunter-gatherers.

Cronus' forceful actions hardened the resilience of the Manus. They resolved to keep sowing the seeds of knowledge among the sparse groups of humans. Their presence also spread the myth of the island of the gods, the cataclysm and the flood into many countries.

The Lyrans flew to Atlantis. They were eager to recreate their anthropological project.

* * *

Cronus was rapturous to find Atlantis relatively unscathed by the deluge. Although the floodwaters had submerged numerous land masses and islands, once the ocean subsided, most places reverted to their original state. Only a few small islands had been destroyed by comet fragments, tsunamis and earthquakes.

He landed in Greater Itza with a substantially upgraded spaceship, unloaded the Hecatonchires, then sent seven original Lyrans in Cyclopes to inspect the terrain.

As a reminder, four of the original Lyrans had been lost. Hyperion and Koios had been killed in the 'war of the gods'. Oceanus and Tethys had disappeared into the ocean. The current crew comprised males Cronus, Iapetus and Krios; females Rhea, Mnemosyne, Themis, Phoebe and Theia. Plus ten 'children of the gods'. All carried desolate memories and scars from the era of Zeus.

You will recall that when a cohort of Lyran scientists arrives on a planet, they generally commit their lives to the research project. Hence, they stay with their genetic experiment and seldom return to their home world. The original team had returned to complete their project.

Also remember, although their physical bodies last about 1,000 years, these intriguing star beings can choose when to die and how to move forward. If they prefer not to transcend to a higher spiritual dimension upon death, they can simply transfer their consciousness to a newly created physical body. Thus they can choose an indefinite physical existence.

The crew reported back with ambivalent news. The Atlantean Empire was a clean slate. All the giants, monsters, therianthropes (Greek, therion 'wild animal', anthropos 'human'), animals and humans had been wiped out. The anthropological experiment would start anew.

The Lyran scientists commenced with replenishing the devastated flora and fauna. Nine Cyclopes were available for travelling to neighbouring continents in search of seeds, bushes, trees and livestock. They also possessed the retrieved repository of seeds and DNA from NaukA.

Cronus in the huge spaceship, and Krios controlling the Hecatonchires on the ground, set about demolishing the Sirian mansions on Tartarus and deliquescing the outlandish gargantuan statues. They were determined to return Atlantis and the islands to their pristine natural state.

As the star beings plunged the depths to survey Avalon, Oceanus and Tethys made a joyful reappearance. They hastily reconvened on the surface and summoned the rest of the crew. It was a heartfelt reunion. In the absence of the Sirians, the two water-gods had re-established dominion over the oceans and rivers. During the cataclysm, destruction of marine life had been minimal. The grotesque creatures of Zeus had been neutered and eventually died. Avalon had been restored to immaculate condition.

Several years passed. The Lyrans' homes and Crystal Temple were exquisitely refurbished. As always, the buildings were designed to integrate and harmonise with the natural environment. All the gods chose to reside on Atlantis (except Oceanus and Tethys). Over the next few decades they would steadily disperse over the rest of the islands.

When construction work in Atlantis was complete, the spaceship (with stowed Hecatonchires) was parked in the renovated storage facility in Tartarus. The Devices of Light (which Zeus had returned before leaving) were also cached here; these included the Diamond Thunderbolt (Vajra) and the Trident. Four Lyrans had been imprisoned in Tartarus, though they had often been allowed to walk outside the volcano under watchful eye of the Sirians. Despite his unpleasant memories, Cronus recreated a protective energy field in the throat of the volcano along with an AI humanoid who stood guard over the spaceship.

The plant and animal life of Atlantis gradually became bountiful. Flowing canals, lush vegetation, cultivated orchards and abundant crops burgeoned across the glorious landscape. The temperate climate and fertile soil also fostered the proliferation of wild orchards bearing delicious fruits.

It would soon be time to reintroduce human beings to Paradise.

* * *

It is not often in life that you get second chances.

Although the Lyrans had made solid ethical decisions the first time, they had absorbed a few ideas from the contrasting actions of the Sirians.

They would start the experiment again, taking it slowly, factoring in natural evolution. However, they would teach extensive skills to the humans, including 'civilised' behaviour like wearing clothes. The secret, they believed for certain, was appropriate and influential role modelling.

Though inherently dispassionate, the Lyrans determined to be more involved with their creation; to 'walk among them' in Paradise. They took inspiration from the mentorship given to the followers of Horus during the time of Zeus. That had fostered a positive outcome.

Over the next decades and centuries, the star beings imported primitive hunter-gatherers from various continents. As before, this resulted in Atlanteans with various skin and hair colour. The consequence of the genetic upgrade created the homogenous blue eyes, supreme health and long life. The life span of altered humans ranged from 300-400 years, some living as long as 500 years.

The Lyrans taught the humans the promised skills: textile fibres, weaving, dyes, pigments, and clothing manufacture; speaking, reading and writing Sanskrit; art and music; mathematics, astronomy, meteorology and geology. The star beings conducted themselves without egotism; hence, those skills were not employed by the Atlanteans for narcissistic purposes, rather for utility, entertainment and joy.

Atlantis became an enhanced version of its previous incarnation.

After much debate, the Lyrans decided to gradually extend their experiment across all the islands east and west of Atlantis, thus recreating the entire Atlantean Empire. However, they would constrain the anthropological upgrades to the imported hunter-gatherers. The rest of the planet would stumble along the path of slow natural evolution.

The phrase 'As above (Atlantis), so below (Avalon)' still applied. Beneath the ocean waves, Oceanus and Tethys altered humans to live comfortably on land and in water. Those beings, named Oceanids, inhabited the underwater city. Oceanids learned Sanskrit but seldom used it; they had been genetically engineered for telepathic communication which was essential for marine living.

During the Lyran absence from Earth, Oceanus and Tethys had continued to create their own children, whom they affectionately called 'water babies' and, as they grew older, 'nymphs'. Nereids (nymphs of the seas) and Naiads (nymphs of fresh water), having witnessed the atrocities of the Sirians, were fiercely loyal to their parents. They were also very secretive, fastidiously avoiding interaction with primitive (non-upgraded) humans.

Life underwater was joyful and serene. Telepathy was the predominant connection among cetaceans (whales, dolphins, porpoises), nymphs and Oceanids. They often roamed the seas and rivers in familial pods, searching for food and playing in the waves. Dolphins were able to store vast amounts of information and often acted as sacrosanct messengers. The bonds forged among cetaceans, nymphs and Oceanids were intense and long-lasting.

As time went by, and the human population burgeoned, leaders were mentored in Atlantis and Avalon to manage mundane anthropological affairs. This delegation of responsibility freed the scientists to focus primarily on research and development. Superlative role modelling, the transmission of ethical codes, and the ostensible distinction between gods and humans, fostered a peaceful and harmonious Atlantean Empire.

Over the subsequent millennia, the Atlantean Empire flourished with abundance and knowledge, while the 'outside world' struggled with day-to-day survival. The Neolithic Revolution (aka Agricultural Revolution), which was the transition of numerous human cultures from a lifestyle of nomadic hunter-gathering to one of agriculture and settlement, gradually spread to many countries. Natural evolution was still a protracted journey.

The resilient and mistrustful Manus (bolstered by the occasional advanced human from Atlantis) carried on their teachings. They also founded various mystery schools and secret societies to preserve their sacred knowledge. Although the title 'follower of Horus' clung to Adhipa in DvAra AreNu, Mesopotamia, the other secret societies used completely different designations. Many of those still exist today.

From the re-entry of the Lyrans in 10300 BC until about 4500 BC, the Atlantean Empire was incongruously juxtaposed with the rest of your planet.

A mover and shaker would be required to impel the next stage of evolution.

One day the luminous hummingbird with green, silver and gold plumage flitted into the Crystal Temple. Cronus glanced up, intrigued at how it had eluded the security system. The hummingbird alighted on the work surface, its inscrutable gaze penetrating the Lyran leader.

I told you at the beginning of this story that we had met before. My identity will soon be revealed. Of course, you have met the hummingbird before too. Are you sensing my esoteric smile?

That hummingbird is an Avatar of the Light. Catalyst of the universe. It likes to flap its wings into established systems, especially ones that are working well. As you can imagine, it is only mildly tolerated by most entities. Fortunately it is exceptionally powerful.

Cronus was informed that change was on the way; another race of advanced beings had been sent; the next level of the anthropological experiment was about to commence; and it was time for planet Earth to evolve.

The Lyran sighed. There was no negotiation or concession.

He stared at the incessant wings, then chuckled.

That darn hummingbird!

* * *

You are going to love this part of your ancient history.

In 4500 BC the Pleiadeans arrived on planet Earth. Despite his unpleasant experience with the Sirians, Cronus was nonchalant about their coming. The Pleiadeans are acknowledged as one of the most advanced races in the galaxy. They are renowned for their spiritual maturity, responsibility and virtue.

The Pleiades is an open star cluster located in the constellation of Taurus. (An open cluster is a group of stars, roughly the same age, held together by mutual gravitational attraction.) The cluster includes over 1,000 hot blue and extremely luminous stars; a few are visible to the naked eye, especially in winter in the Northern Hemisphere. Pleiades (Greek) means 'sailing ones' or 'flock of doves' (rather apt as you will discover).

As with most advanced races, the Pleiadeans have mastered genetics, technology, clean and free energy, propulsion systems, space travel, artificial intelligence (AI) and other scientific disciplines. They are distinguished by their work in analysing, testing and perfecting biological systems.

Pleiadeans are 1.8-metre-tall humanoids, with lithe bodies, white skin, auburn or blonde or white hair, and blue or green almond-shaped eyes. They are trans-dimensional (able to manifest in physical and other dimensions). That means they are not limited to one particular physical form; they can change their appearance at will. Other races often refer to them as the 'shining ones'.

What is the cultural signature of the Pleiadeans? They are the lovers and spiritual teachers of the galaxy. Characterised as mystical, wise, virtuous, peaceful and kind.

The Pleiadeans used instant inter-dimensional transfer of consciousness aka 'jumping' to arrive in Atlantis. No spacecraft or airships required. They landed in Greater Itza as beings of light, carrying no possessions or technology. (Shimmering is often a precursor to 'jumping' and employed as a courteous or considerate gesture.)

Cronus ushered the aliens into the Crystal Temple. He smiled as he heard the tiny wings buzz across the ceiling. Perhaps the Avatar was monitoring the next stage of the evolutionary project.

The team that arrived on Earth comprised: Atlas (leader); males Jahsoes, Quetzalcoatl (my identity is now revealed) and Viracocha; females Pleione, Merope, Electra, Maya, Celaeno, Alcyone, Taygete and Sterope.

You will have noticed that star being exploratory-pioneer crews usually comprise twelve members (2 x sacred numeral 6). Our crew adhered to the universal protocol.

We were given a tour of the Crystal Temple then invited to sit with the Lyrans for one of their lengthy conferences. What they most needed to understand was our intended contribution to the anthropological experiment and our plans for planet Earth.

Cronus graciously offered to let us live anywhere in the Atlantean Empire and to walk among the humans. We agreed to work together to create a superior human by utilising our combined knowledge and mastery of genetic engineering.

Our alliance would naturally be one of peace and love.

Relaxing deep breath ... exhale.

Exciting times lay ahead.

* * *

Let me tell you about our wonderful crew.

Atlas is a natural leader. The commander of our crew and leader of tribes. He is ruggedly handsome with long white hair, moustache and beard, and almond-shaped green eyes. He has the ability to quickly assess people and situations, and devise solid strategies. Although open to debate and discussion, he makes final decisions. We trust him completely.

Pleione is his star mate and counterpoint. Cool and collected in her demeanour, she takes her time assessing people and situations. There is no rush ... she is a treasure trove of information ... and prefers to harvest data from multiple sources. Gentle in spirit, yet determined and resolute, she wields her power in a subtle and resilient manner. Her chosen form manifests shoulder-length white hair and beautiful almond-shaped blue eyes. Certainly not hard to admire. Her speciality is the ancient system of Yoga. (This is the original profound meditative and spiritual practice, not the system of physical exercise popular in your modern world.)

Electra, Maya and Merope have shoulder-length white hair and almond-shaped blue eyes; Celaeno, Alcyone, Taygete and Sterope have shoulder-length auburn hair and almond-shaped green eyes. They adore the multifarious aspects of Nature on different worlds and were eager to commune with the flora and fauna of Earth. The sisters have an exquisite resonance which manifests in music and dance. They love water and prefer being in the vicinity of oceans, rivers and lakes. The Seven Sisters are masters of Magick (or mistresses of Magick).

As your narrator, I am choosing to use Greek substitute names for the above nine Pleiadeans. It will be easier to understand than Sanskrit. It may also help you interpret many of Earth's myths and mysteries.

Viracocha is not a Greek name. It is the legendary name that my Pleiadean brother acquired later on Earth. The epithet applied to this 'god' was Tiqsi Huiracocha (Quechua: tiqsi meaning 'origin, source, root'; huaira or wayra meaning 'wind, air'; cocha meaning 'ocean, lake'). Over time discordant tongues modified this to Ticci Viracocha. Viracocha is a serious and solemn character with long auburn hair, moustache and beard, and almond-shaped green eyes. He bears an onerous responsibility because of his highly developed telepathic, telekinetic and reality-shaping abilities (which can be utilised for mind control). Consequently, he rarely teaches those advanced practices; when he does, it is only to carefully selected Pleiadeans who operate with highest ethics and love.

Quetzalcoatl (pronounced Ketzal-quat) is not a Greek name. It is the legendary name that I acquired during my later adventures on Earth. Quetzalcoatl, or Feathered Serpent, derives from the Nahuatl words quetzal meaning 'emerald plumed bird' and coatl meaning 'serpent'. The epithet arose, in part, from my headdress of quetzal-feathers and my propensity for 'jumping'. The Resplendent Quetzal *(Pharomachrus mocinno)* is a bird with iridescent green plumage that craves freedom (it soon kills itself if placed in a cage). The serpent refers to my skill in navigating the Dreamworld and Astral Planes. As for my physical form, I have long white hair, moustache and beard, with almond-shaped blue eyes.

Finally, there is the mysterious Jahsoes (pronounced Yah-sues), most spiritually advanced of all the Pleiadeans. That is his real name and its origins are obscure. His appearance is striking: pure white hair cascading over his shoulders, white eyebrows, eyelashes and moustache, with almond-shaped blue eyes (the only male of our crew to not have a beard). Jahsoes prefers solitude, spending his days in prayer, meditation and communion with the Source. He says his mission is to explore the depth and extent of Love. Merope was enamoured by Jahsoes' pure energy resonance. She became his soul companion and star mate. Merope shared her knowledge of Magick. Jahsoes ushered her to serene preternatural existence.

The cultural signature of the Pleiadeans rises above our unique personalities and idiosyncrasies. Pleiadeans are the lovers and spiritual teachers of the galaxy. We are mystical, wise, virtuous, peaceful and kind. We tread and reflect the path of Love and Light.

* * *

From 4500 BC we integrated with the Lyrans in Atlantis and Avalon.

After an extensive reconnaissance of the Atlantean Empire, and consultation with Cronus and Rhea, Atlas and Pleione made their home in Lower Itza. Jahsoes and Merope chose to reside on the uninhabited island east of Atlantis (where the Manus had built NaukA before the cataclysm). Viracocha chose an inhabited island to the west of Atlantis.

Electra, Maya, Celaeno, Alcyone, Taygete and Sterope had a very strong bond and decided to live together in the southern part of Atlantis near the smaller volcano. With Lyran permission, the unnamed volcano was designated as Zaila PrIti (Sanskrit, 'mountain', 'love, kindness'); therefore they resided near the Mountain of Love. The mystical females were also keen to visit the intriguing underwater paradise Avalon.

Quetzalcoatl (yep, that's me) negotiated dominion over Poseidia, the large island near present-day Bimini. Each of the Pleiadeans has a different personality. I enjoy leading and positively influencing large tribes. Poseidia had always been a 'secondary' Atlantis and it was agreed that Pleiadean guidance would be beneficial. Although the Lyrans had already renamed the island, I was allowed to conceive a new designation. Considering the verdant gorgeousness, it became Sundara (Sanskrit, 'lovely, charming, beautiful').

Whereas Atlantis was bordered by a ring of protective mountains, Sundara was enclosed by a huge wall inset with platinum (originally built by Poseidon). Hence, the island was still known as the gleaming jewel of the ocean. The lavish Temple of Sundara (previously Temple of Poseidon) was surrounded by concentric rings, traversed by a 9,300-metre-long canal that accessed the ocean.

As a reminder, the temple was surrounded by five sculpted concentric rings of water and land. The innermost islet, bearing the temple, was encircled with a high wall inset with orichalcum, followed by a 500-metre-wide moat. Then a 1,000-metre-wide ring of land, a high wall inset with silver, and another 500-metre-wide moat. Finally, a 1,000-metre-wide ring of land, a high wall inset with gold, and a 500-metre-wide moat.

Cronus had already deliquesced and removed the garish statues in Poseidia, and stripped the orichalcum from the innermost concentric ring and interior of the temple. (Reddish orichalcum was an uncomfortable reminder of the Sirians.) Sundara retained the architectural sophistication without the outlandish embellishments.

After obtaining Lyran consent to replace the orichalcum with a more suitable material, I borrowed a Cyclops to survey the neighbouring continents. Soon a brief mining operation was established using the labour of two Hecatonchires. We extracted emerald from (present-day) Colombia and bluish-green tourmaline from Brazil, and subsequently redecorated the innermost concentric ring and interior of the temple. Sundara emerged viridescent and resplendent. (Green, as you have surmised, is my favourite colour.) The Lyrans were gratified.

* * *

With everyone settled, we commenced work on the anthropological project.

This is the part where we had to be careful. Unlike the Lyrans, and many other advanced races, we were not interested in merely upgrading indigenous inhabitants and perfecting biological systems.

We are motivated by highest ethics and love. Questions we ask ourselves: What is optimal for a species? Where are they in their emotional and spiritual development? Have they embraced virtue, compassion and responsibility? Will an upgrade or intervention cause harm or good?

We had to consider the impact of repatriating altered humans to their original countries; we also had to consider the effect of reinserting significantly altered humans into their original Atlantean tribes. After much debate, we determined to focus on the latter. We would not interrupt the slow natural evolution beyond the Atlantean Empire. Instead, we would effectuate intermittent, cautious and selective upgrading of Atlanteans. This would create a small tier of very advanced humans constrained to Atlantis and Avalon.

Now you may be asking yourself: What is the next stage of evolution?

It is in the direction of the Pleiadeans. As with most evolutionary leaps, it involves treading the path of Love and Light.

The next stage of human evolution is the move from *Homo sapiens* (Latin, 'human', 'wisdom') to *Homo luminous* (Latin, 'human', 'light'). It requires the insertion of Pleiadean DNA into the human genome, and modification of specific genes, thus sparking the transition from 'human of wisdom' to 'human of light'.

Insertion of DNA, especially of the Light variety, can result in disorientation, confusion and a period of adjustment for the organism. Initial, and often long-term, effects may include: a sense of not belonging to your tribe or culture; questions of identity and purpose; a hunger for advanced knowledge; awakening of consciousness; and ascension to a higher dimension. For obvious reasons, we closely monitor upgraded humanoids.

You may have been altered. Are you sensing any effects?

Over the ensuing decades we upgraded a limited number of Atlanteans. These beings, as always, were tall, slender and highly intelligent, with skin of varying colour (originating from different continents). Our intervention produced auburn or blonde hair with green or blue eyes. Those became subtle markers of significantly altered beings.

On the islands of Atlantis and Sundara we created schools to guide these Pleiadean-Atlanteans. Within the Temples we assisted them to develop and manage their burgeoning skills, including clairvoyance, telepathy and telekinesis. We also showed them how to use meditation, prayer, chanting, drumming, dancing, teacher plants and magical cosmic catalysts to attain various states of consciousness and access the multi-dimensions.

As they demonstrated virtue and trustworthiness, the Lyrans allowed the Pleiadean-Atlanteans access to their sacred Stones. This was a huge step for the scientists. Their risk was outweighed by our increased responsibility. Highest ethics and love became crucial. We also had to ensure a level of secrecy and consecrated mindfulness.

As a reminder, the Lyrans used crystals to hold digital information (quantum bits stored and transmitted as pulses of light), for psychic and spiritual purposes (activating the third eye; surfing the multi-dimensions), for local and interstellar communication, for physical and mental healing, and for harnessing and distributing power.

To be clear about terminology, a 'stone' (aka gem, gemstone, jewel, precious stone or semi-precious stone) is a piece of mineral crystal in cut and polished form.

The six-sided Agni ZilA or 'Fire Stone' (aka power crystal) unceasingly absorbed the free energy of the cosmos (when uncovered). Airships, buildings, residences, vehicles, roads and devices were adorned with small crystals that induced power from the Fire Stone. There was a Fire Stone on top of the Crystal Temple in Atlantis and one on top of the Temple of Sundara. The other ten Fire Stones were situated across the Atlantean Empire (including one in Avalon). Fire Stones are large transparent white crystals that glow with a golden light when charged with cosmic energy.

The SaMvAda ZilA or 'Communication Stone' (aka transceiver crystal) is a rose-pink, light-crimson crystal used for local and interstellar communication. One Communication Stone was kept in the Crystal Temple and one in the Temple of Sundara. There other ten were utilised across the Atlantean Empire (including one in Avalon).

The VijJAna ZilA or 'Knowledge Stone' (aka data crystal) is an emerald-green crystal used to hold digital information. Eight Knowledge Stones were stored securely in the Crystal Temple; two were stored in the Temple of Sundara; two were stored in the Temple of Avalon.

The JIvita ZilA or 'Healing Stone' (aka life-force crystal) is an azure crystal which radiates potent energy that dispels pathogens. It is also wielded for cell regeneration and repair, and physical and mental healing. Eight Healing Stones were located in the Crystal Temple; two were located in the Temple of Sundara; two were located in the Temple of Avalon.

The AdhyAtmika ZilA or 'Spirit Stone' (aka transcendence crystal) is a mauve crystal utilised for psychic and spiritual purposes (activating the third eye; surfing the multi-dimensions). Eight Spirit Stones were cached in the Crystal Temple; two were cached in the Temple of Sundara; two were cached in the Temple of Avalon.

Concomitant with their development, the Pleiadean-Atlanteans were given leadership positions in the Atlantean Empire. This required a level of sensitivity and discretion toward their fellow Atlanteans. Public displays of their gifts and powers were discouraged. Following the cultural signature of their 'makers', they engaged mostly in positive role modelling and spiritual teaching.

In a sense, we now had a multi-tiered hierarchy of beings on Atlantis, Sundara and the surrounding islands: Lyran gods, Lyran children of the gods, Pleiadean gods, Pleiadean-Atlanteans, and Atlanteans (and primitive humans on the rest of the planet).

Although peace and harmony prevailed, we kept a close eye on the various beings. Occasional flare-ups occurred, usually due to jealousy or egotism.

As you have probably realised, no one is perfect.

Not even in paradisiacal Atlantis.

* * *

Although not trans-dimensional like us, Pleiadean-Atlanteans lived long physical lives, often up to 700 years. This means they mostly outlived their Atlantean compatriots. Living a long life can create difficulties for romantic relationships.

The Pleiadean-Atlanteans (as with the Lyrans) were taught to keep their genetic code pure, and therefore used spiritual-energetic sex for pleasure, deep connection and intimate consciousness-sharing. That is a beautiful, profound, ecstatic and loving experience. (Tantra, of course, is the foundation for spiritual-energetic sex; however, that belongs to another story.)

They continued their learning in the schools located in Atlantis and Sundara, advancing in knowledge and wisdom as each decade passed. In time, the Lyrans included them in their trips to neighbouring continents to collect primitive humans for importation into the Atlantean Empire. For a while, those expeditions satisfied their curious nature.

Like most advanced beings, the Pleiadean-Atlanteans gradually became frustrated. At a certain evolutionary point, the next phase of development beckons. New challenges, stimulation and learning are required. They began to feel the need to 'stretch their wings', to expand their horizons, to shift their consciousness to the next level.

After a thousand years on Earth, we were beginning to feel the same way. Not because we needed more challenges or exploration (Pleiadeans are able to travel the multi-dimensions). Our concerns pertained to the anthropological experiment. Constraining it to the Atlantean Empire was engendering an unjustified disparity. Why upgrade only a small tier of humans when an entire planet was struggling with painfully slow evolution?

Perhaps we needed to widen the scope of the experiment.

It was a matter we were seriously pondering.

* * *

Remember what I said in the very beginning?

'I am going to tell you a story. An ancient story. A magical history that will resonate in your soul. A history ingrained in your deepest consciousness, in your myths and mysteries. For many of you, it will explain your innermost feelings, longings, reveries and dreams. For some of you, it may evoke a profound and beautiful déjà vu.'

The many eras of the Atlantean Empire will have evoked deep and buried memories. I wonder … Were you incarnated in the Golden Age of Cronus? The Silver Age of Zeus? The enhanced version of Atlantis under the returning Lyrans? The mystical age of the Pleiadeans? Who were you? What kind of being were you? Were you a star being? Was your DNA upgraded by star beings? Were you an imported Atlantean? Were you an Oceanid in Avalon?

Or do you feel that your chapter is still ahead? That the next part of this story will resonate with you?

There is more to discover … to unfold … to reveal.

I sense your innermost smile.

* * *

The Pleiadeans arrived on Earth in 4500 BC. We had become compatriots of the Lyrans, growing deep personal and fulfilling professional relationships. Our values and ethics were similar, engendering mutual respect. 1,400 great years had passed in the Atlantean Empire.

The next crucial year in your ancient history was 3100 BC.

It is interesting how Life works. We had been pondering the extension of the anthropological experiment for some time. The star beings had engaged in many discussions and conferences. Diverse questions required contemplation: Is interruption of natural evolution beneficial for the human race? Who should be upgraded? What level of intervention? What type of accompanying education? How wide the scope? How to instil spiritual values, responsibility and independence?

Concurrently, the Pleiadean-Atlanteans had become frustrated, eager for the next stage of evolution. They wanted more stimulation, learning and challenge. The Atlanteans, too, were hankering for greater knowledge. Everything was pointing to the expansion of the Atlantean Empire.

Let's review the status quo in 3100 BC.

The underwater domain of Oceanus and Tethys functioned peacefully and harmoniously. Their hierarchy was simple and effective. Lyran gods (Oceanus and Tethys), Lyran children of the gods (nymphs), altered humans (Oceanids), plus the beautiful cetaceans (whales, dolphins, porpoises). In truth, the hierarchy was blurred. Nymphs, Oceanids and cetaceans surfed and played together as one deeply connected family. They were intensely loyal to each other, minimising their interaction with surface-dwellers, and living with carefree tranquillity.

The surface of the planet was vastly different. Atlantis, Sundara and neighbouring islands had a multi-tiered hierarchy: Lyran gods, Lyran children of the gods, Pleiadean gods, Pleiadean-Atlanteans (upgraded Atlanteans) and Atlanteans (upgraded humans). Also primitive humans scattered across the rest of the planet. The Lyrans acted mostly as scientists, researchers and mentors. The Pleiadeans took the role of spiritual teachers. Pleiadean-Atlanteans had leadership positions on the various islands. Atlanteans were awkwardly positioned below Pleiadean-Atlanteans yet a few steps above primitive humans. It was that disparity which created (the relatively rare) outbursts of jealousy, egotism and violence.

As I said before, no one is perfect. Every being is evolving emotionally and spiritually.

The island of Sundara was under my authority. It is something that still bothers me. I had taken my crew of eleven Pleiadean-Atlanteans and flown a Cyclops to present-day North America. As with all my expeditions, I had stowed three sacred crystals on board (one Knowledge Stone, one Healing Stone, one Spirit Stone). We had begun reconnoitring the land and initiating plans to upgrade local humans.

One dark night a group of Atlanteans climbed to the top of the Temple of Sundara. They hoped to access the sacred crystal and learn about its power. It was a foolish endeavour that led to a phenomenal disaster.

The group dismantled the protective energy-dome covering the six-sided Fire Stone. The dome had a crucial function: prevent over-charging. It automatically closed when the sacred crystal was 90% charged (thus allowing a margin of safety). The group were unable to achieve their goal and returned to their homes. Unfortunately, the Fire Stone lay exposed for a few days.

Remember, this great crystal, when uncovered, unceasingly absorbed the free energy of the cosmos. As a protective measure, all Fire Stones were connected; they could share excess energy and draw energy from each other. Airships, buildings, residences, vehicles, roads and devices were also adorned with small crystals that induced power from the Fire Stones.

On the fifth day, the exceedingly overcharged Sundara Fire Stone exploded. The enormous excess energy was partially conducted to uncovered Fire Stones in the Atlantean Empire and to local power-inducing crystals. The effects were devastating. The Atlantis Fire Stone, Avalon Fire Stone and three other Fire Stones were overwhelmed and exploded. Most local power crystals also received an intense blast.

Sundara was obliterated and the entire island sank into the ocean, hauling all inhabitants and the temple to a watery grave. The sacred crystals cached in the temple (one Communication Stone, one Knowledge Stone, one Healing Stone, one Spirit Stone) were buried in the melded rubble. You will recall that Sundara was a large island near present-day Bimini. When it sank with all that power and technology it created the mysterious anomaly designated as the Bermuda Triangle.

In Avalon the radical energy penetrated the seismically active Mid-Atlantic Ridge (MAR) running beneath Atlantis. The MAR is a mid-ocean ridge, a divergent tectonic plate boundary located along the floor of the Atlantic Ocean. In the North Atlantic, it separates the North American and Eurasian Plates. The MAR rises 2-3 km above the ocean floor and has a rift valley at its crest marking the location at which the two plates are moving apart (caused by magma rising up the fractures and cooling on the ocean floor to form new ocean floor). Avalon was torn apart; many nymphs and Oceanids perished from the shock waves. Oceanus and Tethys managed to shepherd most of their precious family away from the holocaust. At the request of the Lyran gods, two nearby Pleiadean sisters used their magick to locate and gather the sacred crystals (one Communication Stone, two Knowledge Stones, two Healing Stones, two Spirit Stones).

The combined forces of the Avalon and Atlantis Fire Stone explosions, and the geologically unstable Mid-Atlantic Ridge, caused a violent upheaval in Atlantis. Mount Tartarus (the huge volcano) blew out laterally and collapsed into the sea (submerging the spaceship and Hecatonchires). Mount Love (the smaller volcano) also erupted. The Atlantis land mass broke up into smaller islands. The Lyrans and Pleiadean-Atlanteans scrambled into the Cyclopes. On the ground, two children of the gods and four Pleiadean sisters (using magick) attempted to dampen the formidable energy and retrieve the sacred crystals (one Communication Stone, eight Knowledge Stones, eight Healing Stones, eight Spirit Stones). Although the crystals were salvaged, there were extensive casualties in Atlantis. The deceased included the Lyran gods Krios, Rhea, Mnemosyne and Themis, the two children of the gods, and the majority of Atlanteans.

Viracocha's inhabited island to the west of Atlantis suffered a similar fate to Sundara. Their uncovered Fire Stone exploded, destroying the island which sank into the ocean. As with his Pleiadean brother, Viracocha was away with a crew of eleven Pleiadean-Atlanteans surveying the local human population in present-day South America. When he returned, all that remained was flotsam, volcanic ash and pumice.

As the Greek philosopher Plato later wrote: 'Atlantis perished in a single day and night.' His umbrella statement would be more accurate if reported in this way: 'Vast swathes of the Atlantean Empire perished in a single day and night. Atlantis lost large portions of land to the ocean. Sundara and many smaller islands disappeared.'

It was another sad cataclysmic event in Earth's ancient history.

* * *

Before we move forward in the story, we need an interlude and stocktake.

Lyran gods remaining: (surface) Cronus, Iapetus, Phoebe, Theia, plus eight children of the gods; (underwater) Oceanus, Tethys, plus a multitude of nymphs.

Pleiadean gods remaining: Atlas, Jahsoes, Quetzalcoatl, Viracocha, Pleione, Merope, Electra, Maya, Celaeno, Alcyone, Taygete and Sterope.

Cyclopes remaining: 10 (including the old NaukA)

Sacred crystals remaining: 6 Fire Stones, 11 Communication Stones, 11 Knowledge Stones, 11 Healing Stones, 11 Spirit Stones.

* * *

The gods convened on the northwest coast of Africa (present-day Morocco).

In the sorrowful atmosphere they discussed the strategy for Earth.

The four Lyrans focused on their original projects.

Cronus and Iapetus (each with their own Cyclops and eleven-member Pleiadean-Atlantean crew) determined to monitor the Atlantean Empire; collect all survivors and relocate them to Atlantis; and recover the spaceship and Hecatonchires. They instructed the four male Lyran children of the gods to accompany them. They would keep two Fire Stones, three Communication Stones, three Knowledge Stones, three Healing Stones, three Spirit Stones.

Phoebe and Theia (each with their own Cyclops and eleven-member Pleiadean-Atlantean crew) decided to reinstate their old passion: mentoring the scattered Manus. This would require upgrading of Manu DNA and sharing of sacred knowledge, thereby bolstering the mystery schools and secret societies. The four female Lyran children of the gods, who were previously involved in this project, would accompany Phoebe and Theia. They would keep one Fire Stone, two Communication Stones, two Knowledge Stones, two Healing Stones, two Spirit Stones.

The Pleiadeans enacted a different adventure.

Atlas and Pleione (each with their own Cyclops and eleven-member Pleiadean-Atlantean crew) decided to extend the anthropological experiment, or at least the advanced teachings, into North Africa. Pleione would also keep a close eye on the six sisters, working with them when necessary. They would keep one Fire Stone, two Communication Stones, two Knowledge Stones, two Healing Stones, two Spirit Stones.

The six sisters (Electra, Maya, Celaeno, Alcyone, Taygete, Sterope) opted to spread the advanced teachings throughout the present-day United Kingdom and Mediterranean Europe. Each of the two Cyclopes would carry three sisters with an eleven-member Pleiadean-Atlantean crew. They would keep two Communication Stones, two Knowledge Stones, two Healing Stones, two Spirit Stones.

Viracocha already had a Cyclops and eleven-member Pleiadean-Atlantean crew. He chose to continue the work recently commenced in South America. As with the rest of the Pleiadeans he would ascertain the pertinence of upgrades and spread the advanced teachings. He would keep one Fire Stone, one Communication Stone, one Knowledge Stone, one Healing Stone, one Spirit Stone.

Quetzalcoatl also had a Cyclops and eleven-member Pleiadean-Atlantean crew. He chose to proceed with his plans for North America and Mesoamerica. He would keep one Fire Stone, one Communication Stone, one Knowledge Stone, one Healing Stone, one Spirit Stone.

Despite the cataclysmic destruction of our home, and tragic loss of life, it turns out we were going to expand the Atlantean Empire.

* * *

3100 BC was the beginning of an interesting shift on planet Earth.

A side note for ancient historians: The dispersion of Pleiadeans (and Pleiadean-Atlanteans) explains your present-day archaeologists' reports of the 'unaccountable' birth of civilisation in many parts of the world. This includes Egypt's First Dynasty circa 3100 BC; Indus Valley Civilisation circa 3100 BC (present-day northeast Afghanistan to Pakistan and northwest India); Sumer, Mesopotamia circa 3100 BC (present-day southern Iraq); the founding of Troy circa 3000 BC (present-day Anatolia, Turkey); England's megalithic site at Stonehenge and sacred stone circles at Avebury circa 3000 BC; Scotland's Standing Stones of Stenness circa 3100 BC; Caral, Peru circa 3050 BC (near present-day Lima); and Mesoamerica's Maya Long Count calendar which began in 3114 BC. Many of those civilisations sprang up 'mature' with no evident archaic period.

You will notice in the ensuing chapters that many peoples on the Earth spoke about white-skinned gods arriving on flying ships or gleaming boats. Those myths resulted from the Pleiadean explorers, which is very different to the Flood-and-Ark myth (the two cataclysms of Atlantis were separated by millennia).

Let's begin with my Pleiadean brother Viracocha.

Viracocha (with his eleven-member Pleiadean-Atlantean crew) flew the Cyclops over the north-western section of South America. They had been scanning the area for some time. The silver-grey saucer-shaped airship landed initially in present-day Ecuador, and they gradually worked their way down to present-day Peru, Bolivia, Chile and Argentina.

The Andean cultures all have oral fables about the tall, red-haired, bearded, fair-skinned traveller who arrived from the east. He was known as the 'teacher of all things', bringing to the Andes the gifts of civilisation, including agriculture, mathematics, physics, architecture, engineering, astronomy, meteorology, geology, social organisation, government and a moral code. He was also renowned for healing the sick (by utilising the sacred crystals).

Viracocha and the Pleiadean-Atlanteans were often depicted as bearded men each holding a bag, representing the sowing of seeds (knowledge and agriculture). They were usually considered as 'sorcerers' or 'magicians' by primitive tribes.

Your present-day archaeologists have discovered the Norte Chico civilisation, a complex society located in Caral (north of present-day Lima, Peru). It is the oldest known civilisation in the Americas and one of six sites where civilisation separately originated in the ancient world. Construction of the Pyramids of Caral (where Viracocha later hid the sacred crystals) began in 3050 BC. The Norte Chico cities flourished peacefully for more than 1,200 years.

Subsequent advanced Andean civilisations included the Inca Empire (the political, military and administrative centre was located in present-day Cusco; the empire comprised large parts of present-day Colombia, Ecuador, Peru, Bolivia, Chile and Argentina) and the Muisca (present-day Colombia). Those cultures had myths regarding direct descent from mystical foreigners. The Inca asserted that their god Tiqsi Huiracocha had emerged from Lake Kollasuyu (present-day Lake Titicaca, wherein Viracocha often parked the Cyclops). The name Tiqsi Huiracocha (Quechua: tiqsi meaning 'origin, source, root'; huaira or wayra meaning 'wind, air'; cocha meaning 'ocean, lake') referred both to Viracocha arriving in an airship from across the ocean, and to the magical appearance at the lake. Interestingly, the legendary Inca king Pachakutiq Inka Yupanki, who instructed the building of Machu Picchu, claimed that he was guided by a sacred crystal (retrieved Knowledge Stone).

Viracocha kept secret his highly developed telepathic, telekinetic and reality-shaping abilities (which can be utilised for mind control). He refused to teach those advanced practices to his Pleiadean-Atlantean crew. Few people on Earth know about those skills today.

* * *

Here I am. Some of you have waited a long time to hear my story. Yes, I am smiling again.

Quetzalcoatl (pronounced Ketzal-quat) derives from the Nahuatl words quetzal meaning 'emerald plumed bird' and coatl meaning 'serpent'. The epithet arose, in part, from my headdress of quetzal-feathers and my propensity for 'jumping' (inter-dimensional travel). The Resplendent Quetzal *(Pharomachrus mocinno)* is a bird with iridescent green plumage found from Chiapas, Mexico to western Panama. The serpent refers to my skill in navigating the Dreamworld and Astral Planes. The name Quetzalcoatl, or Feathered Serpent, was acquired during my adventures in Mesoamerica.

Similar to my brother Viracocha, my crew (eleven Pleiadean-Atlanteans) and I had been surveying North America for some time. We were deliberating on the potential for upgrading primitive hunter-gatherers and implementing basic and advanced teachings. When the island of Sundara sank, we committed to the new project.

You might be interested to know that the Pleiadeans adopted a similar dress style to the Lyrans: white robes with azure mantles. We also wore around our necks a conch shell cut at the cross-section, a memento of our Atlantean past.

When we first arrived on the continent we interacted with various North American Indian tribes, located primarily near the south-eastern coast (present-day Virginia, Kentucky, North Carolina, South Carolina, Georgia, Tennessee and Alabama). For that reason Amerindian folklore and legend often mention ancestry and connection to the Pleiades. Later, while working in Mesoamerica, we would regularly return to the North American Indian tribes.

We landed in Mesoamerica in 3114 BC (hence, Mesoamerica's Maya Long Count calendar begins in 3114 BC). Mesoamerica is the region extending from central Mexico through present-day Belize, Guatemala, Honduras, El Salvador, Nicaragua to the north-western border of Costa Rica. History chronicles five major Mesoamerican civilisations: the Olmec, the Teotihuacan, the Toltec, the Mexica (Aztec), and the Maya. Those civilisations consolidated power (with the exception of the politically fragmented Maya) and extended their influence across Mesoamerica in the spheres of politics, trade, technology, art and theology.

Our starting point was the beautiful present-day Yucatan peninsula, home of an indigenous people known as the Maya. As was my custom, I 'jumped' ahead of the Cyclops and greeted the local population. The primitive tribes instantly revered us as gods, sages and magicians. Their tongue soon called me Kukulcan (and later Gukumatz) which roughly translates as 'feathered serpent'.

As with all our projects, we worked cautiously and selectively. Upgrading of indigenous inhabitants' DNA along with higher education tends to engender mixed effects across societies. Experience had taught us the importance of a measured pace. If anything, our mantra was 'slow, slow, slow'.

As the decades passed, we gently disseminated the gifts of civilisation, including agriculture, mathematics, physics, architecture, engineering, astronomy, meteorology, geology, social organisation and government. Crucially, we instilled the

Pleiadean values: virtue, responsibility, compassion, loving-kindness and peace.

Present-day historians assert that Maya civilisation began around 2600 BC and continued until Columbian contact. In truth, it commenced in 3114 BC but we were facilitating a gradual semi-intrusive evolution, which took a long time to manifest.

The territory of the Maya eventually covered a third of Mesoamerica, extending from the present-day Honduras, Guatemala and Belize through the south-eastern states of Mexico. The numerous Maya city-states never achieved political coherence; nonetheless, they exerted an immense intellectual influence upon the other major civilisations in the spheres of mathematics, astronomy, calendars, architecture, art and writing. Mayan hieroglyphic script was the only fully developed writing system of Pre-Columbian Americas; mostly inscribed on stone, pottery, wood or perishable books made from bark paper.

A side note for ancient historians: The sacred Popol Vuh (Mayan, 'Book of the People') is a collection of mythic narratives. One story tells of the Great Father (Cronus) who in the midst of a cataclysm gave the Giron-Gagal (Fire Stone) to the leader of the wise men Gukumatz (Quetzalcoatl). The wise men then sailed (flew the Cyclops) across the ocean to Yucatan. (Those are my translations in brackets.)

With the success of our Maya project, we subsequently turned our attention to the inhabitants of present-day Veracruz and Tabasco. Utilising our distilled learning, we facilitated rapid evolutionary and educational change in the primitive tribes. This civilisation became known as the Olmec. According to your archaeologists, the Olmec mysteriously erupted into mature existence in 1500 BC. In fact, it resulted from the Pleiadean-Atlanteans who introduced agriculture, mathematics, physics, architecture, engineering, pyramid-temples, astronomy, meteorology, geology, social organisation, government and sacred values.

You may be interested to research the 'Man in Serpent' sculpture at La Venta (pre-Columbian archaeological site of the Olmec civilisation located in present-day Tabasco, Mexico). An intriguing relief is carved on a slab of solid granite; the symbol of Quetzalcoatl as Feathered Serpent is crystal clear. The bearded man is carrying the archetypal bag that represents the sowing of seeds (knowledge and agriculture). Similarly, the statue of Viracocha at Tiwanaku in western Bolivia (near the Peruvian border) depicts a bearded man holding the archetypal bag.

We viewed ourselves as catalysts and mentors. Once we had facilitated evolutionary and educational change, we instituted the philosophy of the Atlantean Empire. Selected upgraded humans (whom we still referred to as Atlanteans) were placed in leadership positions, and societies were encouraged to rule themselves. This was meant to foster independence, responsibility and self-sufficiency. We had no interest in being worshipped as 'gods'; being revered as sages and sorcerers was enough.

The Pleiadeans left Earth around 50 BC (more on that later). The civilisations that followed the Olmec were led by the upgraded humans.

Teotihuacan (pronounced Teao-tea-wa-kaan) is both the name of a civilisation and its main city located in the present-day Valley of Mexico, northeast of Mexico City. After the decline of the Olmec, the Teotihuacan dominated during 200 BC - 800 AD, even influencing contemporary Maya civilisation. The city accommodates many architecturally significant Pre-Columbian pyramids, including the Temple of Quetzalcoatl (aka Temple of the Feathered Serpent), the Pyramid of the Sun (third-largest pyramid on your planet) and the Pyramid of the Moon. Teotihuacan is a Nahuatl word meaning 'birthplace of the gods', reflecting mysterious Nahua creation myths. (Those myths originated due to the activities of Quetzalcoatl and the Pleiadean-Atlantean crew.)

The Toltec civilisation (800-1000 AD) was a culture located in Tollan, the present-day Tula Valley, northwest of Mexico City in the state of Hidalgo. Archaeological records are vague and mystical. Some historians believe that Tollan was ruled by Quetzalcoatl, a mysterious godlike being. In truth, the spiritual leader of the Toltec was Ce Acatl Topiltzin, an upgraded human who fastidiously practiced the spiritual values and sacred teachings of Quetzalcoatl (including traversing the Dreamworld and Astral Planes). When the consciousness of Tollan shifted, Ce Acatl Topiltzin and his followers travelled to Chichen Itza (Yucatan) where he was welcomed as a teacher and healer.

As the Toltec civilisation declined, the Valley of Mexico became politically fragmented. A desert people called the Mexica (pronounced Meshica) entered the arena and by 1400 AD were ruling as the head of a Triple Alliance. This alliance comprised their capital city Tenochtitlan (present-day Mexico City) and two other Mexica cities, Texcoco and Tlacopan. The Triple Alliance expanded its empire far beyond the Valley of Mexico, conquering numerous city-states throughout Mesoamerica. At its zenith, the Mexica culture was replete with complex mythological and religious traditions and extraordinary art and architecture. Tenochtitlan was possibly the largest city in the world during this period.

Located at the sacred precinct in Tenochtitlan were several venerated buildings. At the top of the Great Temple or Temple Mayor were two twin temples, one dedicated to Tlaloc, the god of rain, the other to Huitzilopochtli, the god of war. Nearby were the Pyramid of Tezcatlipoca, the Sun Temple of Tonatiuh, and the Temple of Quetzalcoatl. (This typically happened when star beings left a planet. Indigenous inhabitants would create religions and rituals to placate or emulate the missing 'gods'. Sacred values were often discarded in favour of egotism, power and greed.)

Your historians assert that the origin of the Mexica is mysterious. It is said they migrated from a place called Aztlan in the north-western deserts. Before they changed their name to the Mexica they were called the Aztec. It takes only a cursory glance to realise they carried knowledge of Atlantis. Hence, the derivative names Aztec and Aztlan. The language of the Aztec was Nahuatl (pronounced Nah-what). My legendary epithet Quetzalcoatl stems from the Nahuatl words quetzal meaning 'emerald plumed bird' and coatl meaning 'serpent'.

Sadly, once the Pleiadeans left your planet, many human leaders devised political and religious practices that were antithetical to our sacred values. Although they continued to build impressive pyramid-temples (e.g. Mexica in Tenochtitlan; Maya in Palenque and Chichen Itza) the human elite concealed the sacred knowledge and instituted human sacrifice. By controlling the masses through superstition and fear, the rulers were able to accrue political and economic power. Interbreeding (instead of keeping the Atlantean lineage pure) gradually dissipated the divine genetic code. Over the centuries, much of our wonderful work was undone. However, humans were learning through their own choices and consequences. Free will, self-responsibility and independence reigned supreme.

Before we departed from Earth, I buried the sacred crystals in Yucatan (one Fire Stone, one Communication Stone, one Knowledge Stone, one Healing Stone, one Spirit Stone). Unlike the crystals that Viracocha buried, up until today these have not been discovered.

Here comes a shrouded secret. Few people on Earth know that the Pleiadeans will return to your planet. Once you have pushed the limits of egotism, greed, power and destruction, once you have learned the lessons of selfishness and aloneness, once you have united to overcome the dark lattice controlling your world, then we will return and Atlantis will rise. (Such prophecies are embedded in many cultures across your planet.)

So I look forward to meeting you again.

* * *

As fascinating as Earth's ancient history is, many of you are thinking 'Whoa! ... Slow down ... What about the sacred teachings?' Perhaps you are right. Time for a relaxing deep breath ... exhale.

Let's pause the story and share the teachings of Quetzalcoatl. Viracocha refused to reveal his secrets. However, I can share the lessons given to early civilisations in North America, Mesoamerica and South America. Many of those cultures subsequently weaved the sacred knowledge into the 'way of the spiritual warrior'.

I am the master of the Dreamworld and Astral Planes. Here are your lessons in Lucid Dreaming and Astral Travelling.

LUCID DREAMING

What is Lucid Dreaming?

Ordinary dreaming serves various purposes. Reflection on the experiences of waking life. Processing of complex or discomfiting thoughts and emotions. Consolidation of learning and transfer of relevant short-term memory to long-term memory.

During sleep the conscious mind switches off and rests, waking within specific cycles to witness the dream activity of the unconscious mind. The unconscious mind never switches off; it is always 'on duty'. The conscious mind is the tip of an iceberg; the unconscious mind is the rest of the iceberg.

Lucid dreaming is when you (conscious mind) awaken and realise that you are in a dream. Instead of merely being a witness to the unconscious mind's reflection and processing, you are now able to be an active participant. You can dance with the powerful unconscious mind. You can play and learn in this dreamworld.

Benefits of Lucid Dreaming

First of all, it is fun. In a lucid dream, you can do wonderful things like levitate, fly and teleport. You can influence aspects of the dream (depending on the beliefs and limitations of your conscious mind). Glorious landscapes and delightful encounters await you.

On a more serious note, you can use a lucid dream for intrapsychic healing. That means the conscious mind (you) explores and processes information buried in the unconscious mind. Imagine you awaken in a dream and find yourself standing in front of a lovely house. You enter and survey the familiar place. After a while you find stairs that lead to a spacious, dimly lit basement or tunnel beneath the house. There are numerous closed doors down here. You enter one or two rooms and discover interesting items covered in cobwebs. Perhaps you do some cleaning and tidying. Further down the tunnel are more rooms. For some reason those rooms scare you, maybe terrify you. You stand outside the doors, too fearful to enter. Later, feeling a rush of boldness, you sprint to the end of the tunnel and open a huge imposing door. You peek inside and discover an immense spiritual sanctuary, overflowing with sacred energy. You savour it for a while. Eventually you turn and walk back upstairs. Or you wake up in your bed.

The rooms in the basement or tunnel (unconscious mind) contain hidden memories, traumas, taboos, fears and shadows (aspects of you that you prefer not to meet). Healing comes from acknowledging, accepting and compassionately embracing everything you encounter (it's all You). If necessary, you can invoke and channel divine Light into challenging or scary situations.

The spiritual sanctuary is where the soul resides (superconscious mind); it caches past lives and higher knowledge.

A lucid dream offers the opportunity to access fascinating information stored in the unconscious and superconscious minds. This can assist creative thinking, problem solving, deep learning, and emotional and spiritual growth.

You can also plant ideas and train various skills in a lucid dream (which will manifest in your waking life). Your neurological system does not differentiate between waking experiences and lucid dream experiences. How far are you willing to stretch the beliefs and limitations of your conscious mind?

Although you can spontaneously play and flow in a lucid dream, you can also form a plan or strategy prior to entering the dreamworld. While you are awake, write down what you want to experience and achieve, then read it before going to sleep, and enact it in your lucid dream.

Places for Lucid Dreaming

Your bed is the first choice for several reasons. Usually it is very comfortable. It is associated with sleeping and dreaming. You can stretch out and lay on your back. (Although you can lucid dream in any position, it is facilitated by laying on your back, arms by your sides and legs uncrossed.)

Your couch can be a great location for lucid dreaming, provided it is spacious and comfortable. Being alone on the couch means you will not be disturbed by your partner (stealing the covers, rolling over, bumping you, snoring).

Your recliner (reclining armchair) is also an excellent option.

Sleep and Lucid Dreaming

There are two main types of sleep: NREM (non-REM) which is deep, restful and restorative. REM (rapid eye movement) which is active and paradoxical. Most ordinary dreaming and lucid dreaming occur in REM sleep. During REM sleep, muscles in the arms and legs are temporarily paralysed to prevent acting out of dreams.

NREM sleep comprises three stages: N1, N2, N3. As you progress from N1 (brief drowsiness) to N3 (deepest sleep), your brain waves become slower and more synchronised, and your eyes remain still. The sleep cycle (N1) N2, N3, N2, REM repeats throughout the night.

The first part of the night has longer NREM sleep episodes with shorter REM sleep episodes; this switches around in the second part of the night. Hence, most ordinary dreaming and lucid dreaming occur in the second part of the night. The last two hours of sleep consist almost entirely of dreaming (this is prime time for lucid dreaming).

If you take an afternoon nap (30-60 minutes) you will usually enter REM sleep immediately with very little NREM sleep (this is prime time for lucid dreaming).

Preparation for Lucid Dreaming

Practice meditation. There are essentially two types of meditation. Eyes-closed breathing-focused or mantra meditation employed once or twice per day. Eyes-open mindfulness meditation or 'watching the birds in the sky' (as my Pleiadean brother teaches) employed throughout the day. Do the eyes-closed breathing-focused or mantra meditation while laying on your back, arms by your sides and legs uncrossed. This is the same (optimal) position you will use for lucid dreaming. Both types of meditation are useful for the art of lucid dreaming.

Optimise your sleep environment. Ensure you have a good quality pillow and mattress (that suit your body), appropriate level of darkness and quietness, and freedom from disturbances. Minimise your exposure to bright lights and screens close to bedtime (which inhibit melatonin production). Your body responds to amber and red light the same way it does to darkness, so consider those colours for night light.

Research beneficial nutrition. Calcium and magnesium play an important role in healthy sleep. Teas with dream-enhancing effects include Wild Asparagus Root (*Asparagus racemosus*) aka 'the flying herb', Mugwort (*Artemisia vulgaris*) aka 'the dream plant', and Valerian Root (*Valeriana officinalis*) aka 'the sleeping herb'.

Heed sagacious precautions. Caffeine, nicotine, cannabis, alcohol, antibiotics, antidepressants, antihistamines and analgesics are antagonistic to lucid dreaming and astral travelling. Lucid dream-work and astral travelling are contraindicated if you are physically ill or if you are experiencing severe physical or mental health challenges (examples: sleep apnea, anxiety, depression, schizophrenia, bipolar disorder).

Dancing with the Unconscious and Superconscious

The mantra when interacting with your unconscious and superconscious minds is 'dance not dominate'. Those minds are far more powerful and wise than your conscious mind.

Do not try to control or fight the unconscious dreaming mind. Instead, approach it with a friendly collaborative attitude. Remember that the contents of the unconscious mind is You. All the minds are You. It's just that your awareness is usually focused on a narrow field called the Prime Material Plane (the three-dimensional plane in which you live).

The dream is not separate from you. Witness what is being shown to you. Engage the dream with compassionate acceptance and non-judgement. Be kind to all the characters and situations you encounter. This will encourage integration of all aspects of You.

When you do influence the dream, do it respectfully and tenderly.

Ponder the Pleiadean dictum: 'Unconditional love is the true healer.'

Tools for Lucid Dreaming

A crucial prerequisite is Dream Recall. When you get into bed, set an intention and repeat it many times (example: 'I will remember my dreams').

Keep a Dream Diary. The moment you awaken, write down your dreams succinctly in a diary, log book, tablet or computer. Recording your dreams will accentuate their psychological importance.

Over time your diary will reveal personal Dream Signs. A dream sign is a weird or thematic or recurring aspect of a dream experience. List, and regularly update, your dream signs. (Examples: a dancing purple cat; a large golden eye; the sound of rain; unprepared in a school exam room; walking down the street naked; cannot get a digital or electronic device to work; stuck in an elevator; searching for lost possessions; trying to catch a flight.)

Learn to recognise the Dream State. Peruse your list before going to sleep and set the intention to watch for your dream signs. Knowing your dream signs will allow you to identify them in a dream you are witnessing. Then comes the Aha! moment: 'I am awake in a dream'.

You can also use Dream Tests. Practice these when awake so you will remember to do in the dream state: Ask yourself 'Am I awake or dreaming?' then pinch yourself; gaze at the tip of your nose (often not seen in a dream); look at your hand twice and notice if it morphs; read text twice and observe any changes; try to use a digital or electronic device proficiently.

At a Prime Time for lucid dreaming (after waking in the early hours of the morning; prior to an afternoon nap): Set a strong intention, then as you enter the N1 stage of sleep (brief drowsiness) count yourself into dreaming with a Repeated Question (example: one, 'Dreamworld?'; two, 'Dreamworld?', three, 'Dreamworld?'). You may be able to slip straight into a lucid dream.

Try the Alarm Interlude. Set an alarm to wake you two hours before your normal wake-up time. Get out of bed and read a book or update your dream diary for 30-45 minutes. Ensure only dim or red or amber light surrounds you. Then return to bed, reset your alarm (if necessary), speak your intentions, drift back into sleep, and watch for your dream signs. Alternatively, repeat a question or mantra or simply witness the building of the dreamscape, and you may be able to slip consciously into the dreamworld.

* * *

The next teaching is for advanced and adventurous souls.

Lucid Dreaming is a playful, healing and learning experience that takes place *within your own mind*. Your entire consciousness remains within the confines of your physical body. As long as you understand that the conscious, unconscious and superconscious are all You, and you approach all dream aspects with compassion and kindness, you will enjoy safe and wonderful odysseys.

Astral Travelling (aka astral projection) is the *consciousness leaving the physical body* and travelling beyond the Prime Material Plane (the three-dimensional plane in which you live). It only occurs when the mind is awake, not asleep; it is intentional (or by invitation), not inadvertent; and you always remember your astral journeys. Astral travelling carries a whole other level of rewards and risks.

ASTRAL TRAVELLING

What is Astral Travelling?

Astral travelling is an OBE (out-of-body experience). It happens when the entire consciousness (conscious, unconscious and superconscious minds) leaves the physical body.

You need to consider that you incarnated into a physical body on the Prime Material Plane for a reason. You are supposed to be restricted to your 'three-dimensional cocoon' while you learn your life lessons. You chose this part of your journey as a soul.

While residing in this dimension, you have an assigned Guardian, a high-resonance being of light that guards your physical body and soul. You are so used to the Guardian that you are largely unaware of its presence. (For more information about Walkers, Guardians, Messengers and Keepers of the Light, read the book They Walk Among Us.)

You have free will. You are allowed to 'change the agreement' and travel out of your body to explore the astral planes (aka multi-dimensions). The beings of light prefer that you ask them to accompany and guide you. It is not recommended that you travel alone as an unprotected soul (unless you are very experienced and knowledgeable).

Your physical body is kept safe while you are away. Every soul is tethered to a specific body by an 'astral cord'. There are no limits to how far that cord can 'stretch'. No other being can enter your physical body while you are out travelling.

It might be useful to understand that all dimensions are manifestations of the Mind of God (aka the Source). Dimensions are not places but vibrations or resonances that coexist and overlap. Your 'moving and exploring' is actually your consciousness shifting resonances and surfing All That Is.

Try to imagine your journey as conscious mind into unconscious mind (lucid dreaming) into superconscious mind (lucid dreaming) into multi-dimensional Manifested Consciousness (astral travelling into planes of existence or resonances of God) into underlying Unmanifested Consciousness (merging with the Source). (For more information about the Source and multi-dimensions, read the book Star Child.)

Preparation for Astral Travelling

Practice meditation. There are essentially two types of meditation. Eyes-closed breathing-focused or mantra meditation employed once or twice per day. Eyes-open mindfulness meditation or 'watching the birds in the sky' (as my Pleiadean brother teaches in the book I Am) employed throughout the day. Do the eyes-closed breathing-focused or mantra meditation while laying on your back, arms by your sides and legs uncrossed. This is the same (optimal) position you will use for astral travelling. Proficiency in meditation and lucid dreaming is very useful for mastering astral travelling.

Optimise your sleep environment. Ensure you have a good quality pillow and mattress (that suit your body), appropriate level of darkness and quietness, and freedom from disturbances. Minimise your exposure to bright lights and screens close to bedtime (which inhibit melatonin production). Your body responds to amber and red light the same way it does to darkness, so consider those colours for night light.

Research beneficial nutrition. Calcium and magnesium play an important role in healthy sleep. Teas with dream-enhancing effects include Wild Asparagus Root (*Asparagus racemosus*) aka 'the flying herb', Mugwort (*Artemisia vulgaris*) aka 'the dream plant', and Valerian Root (*Valeriana officinalis*) aka 'the sleeping herb'. (It is possible to intentionally move from a lucid dream into an astral journey.)

Choose a comfortable safe place. You need to ensure your body will be secure and content while you are roaming the astral planes. As with lucid dreaming, you can park your body on your bed, couch or recliner. Wear loose clothing or only underwear or be naked. Check that the room temperature is suitable to your needs.

Manage the natural fear. The physical body has a life-preserving instinct and often fights or panics when the soul tries to leave. You need to calm the body with soothing thoughts and assurances that you will return soon. When lucid dreaming, the conscious mind is awake but unaware that the body is paralysed (it is immersed in the dreamworld). When astral travelling commences, the conscious mind is awake and aware that the body is paralysed, which can also cause fear and panic. Meditation practice will assist you to witness, breathe and surrender.

Heed sagacious precautions. Caffeine, nicotine, cannabis, alcohol, antibiotics, antidepressants, antihistamines and analgesics are antagonistic to lucid dreaming and astral travelling. Lucid dream-work and astral travelling are contraindicated if you are physically ill or if you are experiencing severe physical or mental health challenges (examples: sleep apnea, anxiety, depression, schizophrenia, bipolar disorder).

Tools for Astral Travelling

Keep an Astral Diary. The moment you return to your body, write down your astral experience succinctly in a diary, log book, tablet or computer. Recording your location, time, indicators and journey will spotlight patterns and generate ideas for future astral travels.

By interacting with the unconscious mind in a lucid dream (not the contents of the dream but the consciousness behind it) you can request to be shifted to an OBE (out-of-body experience), thus allowing you to commence an astral journey.

You can astral travel at any time, but it helps if your conscious mind is rested. Remember, the conscious mind needs to regularly switch off and recharge. It is part of the entire consciousness that leaves the physical body.

Prime Times for lucid dreaming also apply to astral travelling. The second half of the night, especially the last two hours of sleep; and an afternoon nap (30-60 minutes). Peruse your list of patterns, ask the beings of light to accompany you, lay on your back, prepare your emotions, set a strong intention, invite (or induce) the indicators, and surrender to the experience.

Try the Eyes Open technique. While laying on your back, gently keep your eyes open as long as possible (blinking when necessary) before you succumb to sleep. Often that technique will nudge you into lucid dreaming or astral travelling.

Alternatively, with eyes closed, count with a Repeated Question or mantra (example: one, 'Astral Plane?'; two, 'Astral Plane?', three, 'Astral Plane?'). That may shift you to an OBE (out-of-body experience), allowing you to commence an astral journey.

Use the Alarm Interlude. Set an alarm to wake you two hours before your normal wake-up time. Get out of bed and read a book or your astral diary for 30-45 minutes. Ensure only dim or red or amber light surrounds you. Then return to bed, reset your alarm (if necessary), lay on your back, prepare your emotions, set a strong intention, invite (or induce) the indicators, and surrender to the beings of light.

If you awaken spontaneously in the middle of the night (and you don't need to use the bathroom) you can sometimes consciously and intentionally shift into astral projection. As always, lay on your back, prepare your emotions, set a strong intention, invite (or induce) the indicators, and surrender to the beings of light.

Occasionally you may experience sleep paralysis as you wake in the morning. If you have no family or work or school responsibilities, and no impending alarm, you can sometimes consciously and intentionally shift into astral projection.

Indicators of Astral Travelling

There are signs that astral projection is imminent. These occur when the soul is getting ready to exit the body (whether intentionally or by invitation of higher beings).

For most of you these indicators will be starkly familiar. It will probably be a relief to understand some of your mysterious and frightening experiences.

Body Paralysis occurs during both lucid dreaming and astral travelling. It can be very scary if you do not know about this natural protective mechanism (which prevents physical acting out of dreams and astral journeys). You should expect body paralysis. Learn to witness, breathe and surrender. Be positive when it occurs because an astral door is opening.

Clairvoyant Experiences. Your consciousness shifts to a higher frequency prior to astral projection. Although beings of light are often around you, suddenly your body is paralysed and you are sensing those beings with crystal clarity. If you misunderstand this natural phenomenon it can be terrifying. Sometimes you feel an entity moving on your bed, or a hand touching your chest (coaxing the soul to exit), or you see ethereal lights glimmering around you, or you hear a whispered message in your ear. Once again, witness, breathe and surrender (skills you learned from meditation). Ask the beings of light for solace and guidance.

Tingling Sensations. Wonderful high-resonance energy flows into your soul to shift it to a higher frequency. This intense 'electric' sensation may surge through your chest or along your body. It is sometimes accompanied by a high-pitched buzzing noise and brilliant white light.

Astral Vision. Despite your physical eyes being closed, you are able to see the Prime Material Plane (examples: your bedroom or lounge). This is a clear sign that astral projection is imminent.

Once you are able to calmly embrace those indicators, you can practice inducing the sensations into your being. This will allow you to intentionally raise your vibration, giving you more control over astral experiences. You will be able to choose when to leave your body. As always, it is strongly recommended that you ask the beings of light for protection and guidance.

You may have overcome your fear and embraced those intense indicators, yet you have never experienced an astral journey. There is a simple reason for this. Free will. All the indicators are merely a 'warm-up' or precursor to astral travelling. Astral projection is not something that happens to you. You have to make the move. You have to get out of your body.

How to Get Out of Your Body

Before we discuss the methods for exiting your body, consider your body's position on the bed, couch or recliner. The optimal position for astral projection is laying on your back, arms by your sides and legs uncrossed. Apart from being a very comfortable position, most people project upwards, so it will feel natural to float up and out of your body. Laying on your stomach means you're either going to project down through your bed or out of your back (which is sometimes disconcerting).

Teleporting is the quickest easiest exit. Use your will and intention (your most important astral tools). Choose a location in the room or nearby your home. You can use the same destination every time. When you arrive take a few moments to settle.

Rolling is the second fastest way. When you awaken with body paralysis, just roll your astral body off the side of your bed. Similar to teleporting, your entire astral body is coming out at the same time, minimising any resistance from your physical body. As soon as you have exited, you can shift to another dimension.

Rising is the slow cautious method. When you awaken with body paralysis, try to lift your physical arms. You will see (astral vision) or sense your astral arms rising. Ignore any pulling sensation from your physical body. Then sit up with your astral body and climb out (or stand up). To confirm your exit, glance down at your physical body still laying on the bed.

Sinking is the opposite of rising. Presuming your physical body is in the optimal position, you are sinking your astral body out the back (and probably through your bed and floor). This may be slightly easier than rising out. (Although in the beginning it is sometimes disconcerting to move through your bed and floor.)

Ask the beings of light for assistance in leaving your body. It is highly recommended that your entire astral experience takes place under the guidance, protection and mentorship of the wonderful beings of light.

Travelling the Astral Planes

When you first start astral travelling you will probably need a period of orientation. Your astral senses may seem acute. Take it slow and easy. Be kind and gentle with yourself. Try to moderate your emotions, as intense emotions (e.g. fear, excitement) can propel you back into your physical body. As usual, remember to witness, breathe and surrender (skills you honed during meditation).

Everything beyond the limited Prime Material Plane operates with thought-force. This is a combination of will and intent. If you want to meet someone (e.g. deceased relative) or visit a place, simply use your thought-force.

Astral travelling is restricted or expanded by your beliefs. Liberate your mind. Who would you like to see? Where would you like to go? Why walk when you can fly? Why fly when you can teleport? Experiment and be confident. Practice using your thought-force. Like every skill, improvement comes from patience and practice.

There is one caveat. Your consciousness vibrates with a particular resonance which will allow or deny you entrance to certain astral planes (aka multi-dimensions). Resonance is based on your current state of evolution, as well as your beliefs and attitudes. While evolution is an ongoing process (naturally restricting aspects of your journey) you do have control over your beliefs and attitudes.

The following are relevant and significant excerpts from the book The Fractal Key:

'You are consciousness. You are a transmitter and receiver of consciousness. You are swimming in a sea of consciousness. Your beliefs, stories and ideologies restrict your transceiver … sometimes your beliefs and fears get in the way … you are creating (or experiencing) your reality by your perceptions, choices and beliefs.'

'There are many worlds beyond this one. Multitudinous dimensions. Infinite possibilities. Your mission is to follow the rays of light and go Home. As you proceed up the Sacred Ladder, you will occasionally encounter dark beings who tempt you with alluring propositions. Beware. The nature of the dark side is conceit, deceit and disconnection. It takes you further and further from the Source until the agony becomes excruciating. And it's a long road back.'

'Not all higher-dimensional beings are welcoming or interested in visitors. Some blatantly ignore you or merely tolerate your presence. Others assist with loving-kindness and teachings. A few may mentor you. You learn to navigate to the optimal realms.'

'The secret is to align yourself with the beings of light that exist in the multi-dimensions. Walk with impeccability, altruism and radical respect. Do no harm and accept no harm.'

Hopefully you will be travelling the astral planes under the (requested) protection and guidance of the beings of light. Keep in mind that you can invoke divine Light (the Source) to shield you whenever you feel threatened. You can also invoke divine Light to shield your physical body before you leave (it can give peace of mind). You can channel divine Light into any situation or being you encounter in the multi-dimensions.

Although you will mostly be surfing the 'spatial' dimensions, you can also travel through time. Such an advanced journey results from intense thought-force and plenty of practice.

How to Return to Your Body

If you left your body in a comfortable safe place, it should be waiting contentedly for your return.

Although no being can inhabit or possess your body while you are away, on rare occasions you might return and find a low-resonance being loitering near your body. Use a confident thought-force and order it to leave. Alternatively, channel divine Light into the entity; it will soon scurry away. If you have followed the recommendation to travel under the guidance and protection of the beings of light, you should never encounter such a situation.

Teleporting. Use your thought-force (will and intention). Think about being back in your body and you will instantly be there.

Flying. Fly to your body, lay down on top of it, and merge into it.

Falling. From high in the sky or other lofty vantage point, simply let go and fall. Falling backwards is very effective. You will move rapidly into your body.

Ask the beings of light for assistance in returning to your body. You will find yourself immediately back in your body.

Once you have returned to your body, you may awaken, slip into a lucid dream or fall deeply asleep. The latter is most likely because astral travelling expends some of your mental energy.

Remember to thank the beings of light for their guidance, protection and mentorship. This will assure you of many future enjoyable astral adventures.

* * *

As your final lesson, let me briefly explain the power of teacher plants and cosmic catalysts. Viracocha and I lectured about these natural wonders in the early civilisations of South America, North America and Mesoamerica. Over the millennia, of course, primitive hunter-gatherers across the planet had stumbled across these intriguing flora. Shamanism (and the use of teacher plants) is therefore an age-old practice.

TEACHER PLANTS AND COSMIC CATALYSTS

The following are relevant and significant excerpts from the book The Fractal Key:

'Psychedelic means 'mind-manifesting' and entheogen means 'meeting the divine within'. Entheogen is the preferred term as it denotes the sacredness of the journeys. Psychedelics and entheogens retune your awareness to the vast array of multi-dimensional consciousness, to the infinite layers and levels of the Source.'

'Entheogens retune your transceiver, first temporarily then permanently. They break open the restricting barriers and perspectives and show you the other television channels. As always, this is moderated by your readiness and resistance. Entheogens merely extend an invitation. Sometimes your beliefs and fears get in the way and you refuse to watch a particular channel. When that happens, the higher beings disengage and patiently wait.'

'Entheogens and intent are utilised to shift the assemblage point. This is a gradual process requiring dedication, time and patience. Once the assemblage point is stabilised in a new position, you operate in a different reality. You no longer need entheogens.'

The important point is that teacher plants and cosmic catalysts can facilitate and expedite both lucid dreaming and astral travelling. It is absolutely essential, however, that journeys with teacher plants or cosmic catalysts are only done under the guidance, protection and mentorship of highly experienced ethical shamans, psychologists or psychiatrists.

For the complete lessons on teacher plants, cosmic catalysts, consciousness-shifting, healing and transcendence, plus precautions and caveats, read the book The Fractal Key.

Wishing you many wonderful journeys.

* * *

It's time to get back to the story.

While Viracocha and his crew were working in South America, Quetzalcoatl and his crew were sowing the seeds of enlightenment in North America and Mesoamerica.

Do you recall the choice of my six sisters?

Electra, Maya, Celaeno, Alcyone, Taygete and Sterope opted to spread the advanced teachings throughout the present-day United Kingdom and Mediterranean Europe. Each of the two Cyclopes carried three sisters with an eleven-member Pleiadean-Atlantean crew. They held two Communication Stones, two Knowledge Stones, two Healing Stones, two Spirit Stones.

The sisters adopted the same strategy as the rest of the Pleiadeans. Intermittent, cautious and selective upgrading of local hunter-gatherers' DNA along with slow and steady dissemination of the gifts of civilisation (agriculture, mathematics, physics, architecture, engineering, astronomy, meteorology, geology, social organisation, government and a moral code). Similar to their brothers in the Americas, the sisters became renowned for healing the sick (by utilising the sacred crystals).

Most importantly, they instilled the Pleiadean values: virtue, responsibility, compassion, loving-kindness and peace.

The Pleiadean-Atlantean influence was felt in the United Kingdom (England, Wales, Scotland, Ireland) and Mediterranean Europe (Portugal, Spain, France, Italy, Greece). Evidence remains in the form of England's megalithic site at Stonehenge and sacred stone circles at Avebury constructed circa 3000 BC, and Scotland's Standing Stones of Stenness built circa 3100 BC. Your archaeologists have discovered many other related sites in Europe, for example the Minoan civilisation on the island of Crete and other Aegean islands circa 3100 BC. The famed Pythia, aka the Oracle of Delphi (prophetic High Priestess), was connected to the Pleiadean-Atlanteans. Interestingly, Delphi is derived from the Greek word delphis meaning 'dolphin', a clear connection to Atlantis.

As always, the Pleiadeans and Pleiadean-Atlanteans were considered as 'sorcerers' or 'magicians' by primitive tribes. In the United Kingdom and Mediterranean Europe this was amplified because my sisters are masters of Magick. Their teachings engendered a special kind of history.

I sense you would like more details. It is very important that you focus on the original Pleiadean spiritual teachings. Also, keep in mind our sacred values.

MAGICK

What is Magick?

Magick is the science and art of manifestation in conformity with Will and Intent.

The spelling of that word is used to differentiate the occult from performance magic (trickery, sleight-of-hand, stage magic).

Occult comes from the Latin word occultus meaning 'hidden, concealed, secret'. It therefore refers to 'knowledge of the hidden' or 'knowledge of Reality beyond the Prime Material Plane'. The word occult has nothing to do evil or dark energy (a later superstitious corruption of its meaning).

This is an opportune time to refresh your mind: read the Consensual Reality and VIKAR teachings in the book Heart Song; and read the Creation, Wills and Flow lesson given by the Artisan in the book 5D.

Magick (aka Sorcery) is practiced by a magickian (aka a sorcerer). Magick is the wielding of consciousness and energy to create and manifest realities, ideally in synchronisation with high-resonance beings of light and the Source.

Tools for Magick

Purification is the preparation of body and mind prior to spiritual practice (or event or ceremony). It may involve fasting, a special diet, sexual abstinence, bathing, prayer or meditation. Shamans often insist that attendees follow particular diets and sexual abstinence prior to entheogen journeys. Many spiritual systems have strong views regarding physical purity. Here is an excerpt from the book The Tribe: 'Tantrikas keenly respect the human body, regarding it as a holy temple of the soul. There is, at minimum, a fastidious focus on optimal nutrition and avoidance of pollutants. If you want to experience Tantric ecstasy, you need to abstain from all dietary stimulants. Your body is a finely tuned temple with the capacity for phenomenal pleasure and physiological bliss. Your body contains the foundation for emotional and spiritual ecstasy.'

Banishing is the removal of energy (and consciousness) that might interfere with the sorcerer or sorcery. It can be implemented at any time; however, it is mostly utilised prior to an event or ceremony. Banishing is performed on a venue, a magick circle, and attendees at a ceremony. After negative energy and entities have been dispelled, high-resonance energy and entities are requested as a protective shield (around the sorcerer, venue, circle, attendees).

It is reminiscent of the ancient shamanic practice. Here is an excerpt from the book The Fractal Key: 'Before commencing an entheogen journey always clear your chakras and energy field then seal them in Light. You also need to clear the energy of the journey venue and seal it in Light. Once that is complete you invite the presence of the beings of light.'

A magick circle is a demarcated circle or sphere that forms a sacred space and holds sacred energy. It may be drawn physically (using salt, chalk or cord) and/or energetically (using will and intent). Magick circles and sacred spaces are employed in Shamanism, Sorcery and other spiritual systems.

Consecration is the dedication of a symbol, instrument or space to a specific spiritual purpose. It requires the focusing of will, intent and energy. Examples include pentagrams, hexagrams and magick circles (Sorcery), mesas (Shamanism), mandalas (Hinduism and Buddhism), yantras (Tantra and Hinduism), amulets, talismans, crystals, stones and statuettes.

Invocation is inviting, calling in or identifying with a spiritual being. This is performed for protection, guidance and mentorship. It is recommended that you invoke your soul (superconscious mind), high-resonance beings of light or the Source. Invoke in a tone of sacredness and respect.

Evocation is commanding, channelling or sending energy or entities. The sorcerer uses a wand, staff, incense, fire, drawing of diagrams or casting of spells (verbal ritualised evocation). That depends on the symbols and instruments that have been consecrated.

True Power in Magick

While there is great value in consecration (e.g. creating magick shortcuts; expediting invocations and evocations) all symbols, instruments, rituals and incantations are intermediate devices. They reside between the sorcerer and energy.

The Pleiadean rule is: 'Faith guides intention. Intention guides energy.'

Less evolved and inexperienced beings put their faith in intermediate devices. Those devices work because faith guides intention, and intention guides energy.

Advanced beings eschew intermediate devices and use faith directly.

As the Crystal Shaman teaches in the book The Fractal Key: 'The secret, my protégés, is to keep the power within you. No need for external tools and devices. Be real. Be free.'

Light vs Darkness

In all spiritual systems and aspects of life, you have a fundamental choice. To walk toward the Light or away from the Light (into the Darkness). The consciousness behind that choice is always Love.

You can use magick to harm other beings, accrue power and resources, self-aggrandise, travel the low-resonance planes and connect with dark entities.

You can use magick to help other beings, benefit your planet, spread joy and peace, travel the high-resonance planes and connect with beings of light.

Magick is a neutral power. Manifestation depends on will and intent.

Heed the Pleiadean values: virtue, responsibility, compassion, loving-kindness and peace.

Heed the shamanic values: impeccability, altruism and radical respect.

This is not for karma. Karma is just a red flag offering a course-correction.

This is about choosing Love.

Walking the path of Light.

Returning to the Source.

* * *

You may be wondering what happened to our paradisiacal home. Here comes a brief flashback.

The combined forces of the Avalon and Atlantis Fire Stone explosions, and the geologically unstable Mid-Atlantic Ridge, caused a violent upheaval in Atlantis. Mount Tartarus (the huge volcano) blew out laterally and collapsed into the sea (submerging the spaceship and Hecatonchires). Mount Love (the smaller volcano) also erupted. The Atlantis land mass broke up into smaller islands. The Lyrans and Pleiadean-Atlanteans scrambled into the Cyclopes. On the ground, two children of the gods and four Pleiadean sisters (using magick) attempted to dampen the formidable energy and retrieve the sacred crystals (one Communication Stone, eight Knowledge Stones, eight Healing Stones, eight Spirit Stones). Although the crystals were salvaged, there were extensive casualties in Atlantis. The deceased included the Lyran gods Krios, Rhea, Mnemosyne and Themis, the two children of the gods, and the majority of Atlanteans.

Vast swathes of the Atlantean Empire perished in a single day and night. Atlantis lost large portions of land to the ocean. Sundara and many smaller islands disappeared.

Cronus and Iapetus (each with their own Cyclops and eleven-member Pleiadean-Atlantean crew) determined to monitor the Atlantean Empire; collect all survivors and relocate them to Atlantis; and recover the spaceship and Hecatonchires. They instructed the four male Lyran children of the gods to accompany them. They kept two Fire Stones, three Communication Stones, three Knowledge Stones, three Healing Stones, three Spirit Stones.

It took a few weeks to gather the surviving Atlanteans and transfer them to the Islands of Atlantis. The newly named Islands of Atlantis were all that remained of the original Atlantis land mass.

While Iapetus and the four children of the gods worked on recovering the sunken spaceship and Hecatonchires, Cronus surveyed the Islands for two lofty locations to install the Fire Stones.

No one really knows what happened. What caused the spaceship to explode and destroy the Cyclops? Was it an aftershock in Avalon? Did the shattered Avalon or Atlantis Fire Stones still carry excess charge? Was it connected to the instability of the Mid-Atlantic Ridge?

For Cronus it was the emotional last straw. He had lost his partner Rhea in the recent apocalypse. Now Iapetus and four children of the gods were gone. The tragedy cut his heart, overwhelming him with grief and anger. The once dispassionate star being would be forever transformed.

Cronus offered his crew the Cyclops and freedom. After much pleading and cajoling they finally relented. The eleven Pleiadean-Atlanteans decided to rebuild Atlantis and govern the approximately five hundred Atlanteans spread across the Islands. For that reason, Cronus bequeathed to his crew two Fire Stones, two Communication Stones, two Knowledge Stones, two Healing Stones, two Spirit Stones.

After scanning the locations of the Lyrans and Pleiadeans, Cronus asked to be deposited in present-day Egypt. No one was there and he wanted to be alone. His crew bade him farewell in Lunu, located at the beginning of the Nile Delta in Lower Egypt (Northern Egypt). He retained one Communication Stone, one Knowledge Stone, one Healing Stone, one Spirit Stone.

Cronus was torn by sadness, guilt and anger. He needed a respite from the chaos. He needed time to process his thoughts and emotions. Contrary to his disposition, he turned away from genetics and anthropology, instead immersing himself in art and pottery. It was a new field in which he had little experience.

However, the vocation would be suitable, allowing him plenty of time for quiet reflection.

Over the ensuing decades the Lyran star being developed numerous tools and techniques. His studio, recessed in a dark alley, soon displayed an array of stone statues, fine reliefs and sumptuous pottery. Similar to his magnificent pots and urns, Cronus was being hardened and burnished in the fires of Life.

He stayed in contact with Phoebe, Theia, the Pleiadeans and his Pleiadean-Atlantean crew (using the Communication Stone) and acquiesced to occasional visits, but Cronus remained concealed as a 'human artist' in Lunu for a very long time.

* * *

While Viracocha was touring South America, Quetzalcoatl was working in North America and Mesoamerica, and Electra, Maya, Celaeno, Alcyone, Taygete and Sterope were traversing the United Kingdom and Mediterranean Europe.

Atlas and Pleione (each with their own Cyclops and eleven-member Pleiadean-Atlantean crew) decided to extend the anthropological experiment, or at very least the advanced teachings, into North Africa. They would commence in present-day Morocco and hug the Mediterranean coastline all the way to Egypt. The proximity to Mediterranean Europe would allow Pleione to keep a close eye on the six sisters, working with them when necessary. Atlas and Pleione kept one Fire Stone, two Communication Stones, two Knowledge Stones, two Healing Stones, two Spirit Stones.

You will recall that Atlas is a natural leader. The commander of our crew and leader of tribes. He is ruggedly handsome with long white hair, moustache and beard, and almond-shaped green eyes.

He has the ability to quickly assess people and situations, and devise solid strategies. Although open to debate and discussion, he makes final decisions. We trust him completely.

Pleione is his star mate and counterpoint. Cool and collected in her demeanour, she takes her time assessing people and situations. There is no rush ... she is a treasure trove of information ... and prefers to harvest data from multiple sources. Gentle in spirit, yet determined and resolute, she wields her power in a subtle and resilient manner. Her chosen form manifests shoulder-length white hair and beautiful almond-shaped blue eyes. Certainly not hard to admire. Her speciality is the ancient system of Yoga. (This is the original profound meditative and spiritual practice, not the system of physical exercise popular in your modern world).

Atlas and Pleione followed the same strategy as the rest of the Pleiadeans. Intermittent, cautious and selective upgrading of local hunter-gatherers' DNA along with slow and steady dissemination of the gifts of civilisation (agriculture, mathematics, physics, architecture, engineering, astronomy, meteorology, geology, social organisation, government and a moral code). They also instilled in the local populations the Pleiadean sacred values: virtue, responsibility, compassion, loving-kindness and peace.

Although Atlas and Pleione were partners, they were mature enough to spend time apart fulfilling overarching missions. Atlas stayed in regular communication with the Pleiadeans, and often flew to the Americas to monitor the work and progress of Viracocha and Quetzalcoatl. Atlas employed a 'loose leadership' style: he neither micromanaged nor dictated the methods of operation; instead, he laid the framework of sacred values and strong ethics, shared his advanced knowledge and wisdom, empowered his compatriots, and expected superlative results.

When not working with Atlas, Pleione spent time with the six sisters across the pond (Mediterranean Sea). Apart from her other wonderful qualities, Pleione was dedicated to the consciousness of the Divine Feminine and the sacredness of Nature. The consequence of magickal female Pleiadean energy, along with alignment to the Divine Feminine and deep respect for Nature, engendered a distinctive and exquisite consciousness throughout the United Kingdom and Mediterranean Europe. Sadly, centuries after the Pleiadeans left your planet, those beautiful teachings were corrupted and vilified. During recent decades the magickal female consciousness is slowly re-emerging in your world.

As a variation on the cultural archetype established in the United Kingdom and Mediterranean Europe, Pleione and her crew regularly flew to present-day northwest India. Here they not only implemented the selective upgrading of local hunter-gatherers' DNA and slowly disseminated the gifts of civilisation, they also instituted and taught her speciality: the ancient system of Yoga. A contrasting yet equally elegant cultural archetype was steadily cultivated. As always, the local anthropological experiment was imbued with the Pleiadean sacred values.

* * *

It would be remiss of me not to place a bookmark here. No doubt, your interest is piqued.

Let me introduce the ancient system of Yoga.

YOGA

What is Yoga?

Yoga (Sanskrit, 'yoke, concentration, union') consists of spiritual and mental practices that facilitate the states of liberation, bliss and enlightenment. A dedicated practitioner of Yoga is called a yogi.

Benefits of Yoga

The meditation aspect assists with 'watching the birds in the sky' or noticing the near-constant thoughts that flit across the mind. With application of eyes-open and eyes-closed meditation techniques you can gradually set yourself free from thoughts and discover pure consciousness.

As you discover your true nature, and your consciousness expands, you will experience a beautiful oneness with all beings and things. This state generates an exquisite peace.

The next level involves the dissolution of self and merging into Self. It is accompanied by ecstasy and bliss. You flow through Love into Light. You realise the Unmanifested Consciousness (aka the Source). You experience enlightenment.

Mastery of the levels and layers of consciousness opens the doors to supernatural and preternatural abilities, although those become insignificant and paltry compared to the states of bliss and enlightenment.

Transcendental Goals of Yoga

The penultimate goal of Yoga is mokSa aka mukti (Sanskrit, 'liberation'). This refers to (a) freedom from ignorance and limited knowledge (b) freedom from the deluge of thoughts and 'monkey mind' (c) freedom from saMsAra (Sanskrit, 'transmigration, cycle of existence') which is repeated incarnation in various (especially lower) planes of existence.

The ultimate goal of Yoga is nirvANa (Sanskrit, 'disappear, extinguish, union with Supreme Spirit'). This refers to the realisation that self does not exist, and that everything is Self or God or the Source. Bliss and ecstasy are natural companions of this state of enlightenment.

Tools for Yoga

The Yoga taught by Pleione employed spiritual and mental practices to reach the transcendental goals. There were no physical strengthening and flexibility exercises; such Asanas (Sanskrit, 'postures') were invented thousands of years later, and have nothing to do with the original teachings.

VijJAna-Yoga (Sanskrit, 'knowledge, wisdom') aims to achieve mokSa (Sanskrit, 'liberation') through freedom from ignorance and limited knowledge. This Yoga is about penetrating the mystery of reality and absorbing the advanced teachings. (It is recommended that you read the books The Other Side and Star Child.)

RAja-Yoga (Sanskrit, 'sovereign, king') aims at liberation through meditation. The intention is freedom from the deluge of thoughts and 'monkey mind'; then discovery of your true nature and expansion of consciousness. There are essentially two types of meditation. Eyes-closed breathing-focused or mantra meditation employed once or twice per day. Eyes-open mindfulness meditation or 'watching the birds in the sky' (as my Pleiadean brother teaches in the book I Am) employed throughout the day.

Meditation is a personal decision that results from discussion with the yoga teacher. You need to choose a practice that feels comfortable and works for you. You may even have access to modern neurofeedback devices that enhance and expedite meditative states.

Mantra-Yoga (Sanskrit, 'magical prayer, incantation') aims at liberation through the repetition (mental or aloud) of magical sounds. Universal mantras (e.g. 'aum', the primordial vibration) or a secret mantra (unique to the individual) may be given by the yoga teacher.

Bhakti-Yoga (Sanskrit, 'devotion, adoration') aims at liberation through surrender of self and immersion into the Divine. This

Yoga is focused on the cultivation of love and devotion toward God aka the Source.

Karma-Yoga (Sanskrit, 'action') aims at liberation through losing your self in service to others. This is essentially love in action. (It is recommended that you read the book They Walk Among Us.)

Tantra-Yoga (Sanskrit, 'weave, system, mystical formula') aims at liberation through subtle energy work, raising the resonance of chakras, uncoiling Kundalini, and shifting perception into transcendental reality. (It is recommended that you read the books Star Child and The Tribe.)

Embrace Sacred Values. Embrace the Pleiadean values: virtue, responsibility, compassion, loving-kindness and peace. Heed the shamanic values: impeccability, altruism and radical respect. Allow those values to guide your thoughts, words and behaviour.

Choose Love and Light. Choose to Love. Walk the path of Light. Make an allegiance with the high-resonance beings of light. Contemplate your ultimate destination: return to the Source.

Siddhis of Yoga

Mastery of the levels and layers of consciousness opens the doors to supernatural and preternatural abilities. These siddhis (Sanskrit, 'bliss, attainment, perfection') or mystical powers are a natural result of reaching advanced states of consciousness. Abilities may include clairvoyance, precognition, telepathy and telekinesis. If your resonance shifts high enough you may manifest invisibility, levitation and translocation, although it often becomes difficult to remain on the Prime Material Plane at this stage.

An advanced yogi will refuse to identify with siddhis, as that may encourage egotism and arrogance, creating a detour on the path to awakening and enlightenment. Equally, a yoga master will never display mystical powers when challenged or for the amusement of others, as that distracts from the ultimate goals of mokSa and nirvANa.

Teacher of Yoga

When it comes to Yoga, Magick and Shamanism, it is best to engage the services of a highly experienced ethical mentor. The nature of those spiritual systems means you will benefit from the guidance and protection of a high-level teacher. Also, secret mantras, advanced techniques and esoteric teachings are never published, rather they are handed down by direct face-to-face transmissions.

* * *

Atlas and Pleione extended the anthropological experiment, disseminated the advanced teachings, and cultivated exquisite cultural archetypes along the North African coastline culminating in Egypt, and in the Indus Valley.

Your archaeologists are yet to discover evidence of the 'lost civilisation of Atlantis' in Morocco. The intriguingly named Atlas Mountains are a mountain range extending approximately 2,500 km through present-day Morocco, Algeria and Tunisia. Numerous archaeological sites, including those in Mohenjo-daro and Harappa in Pakistan, attest to advanced cultures established in the Indus Valley. Indus Valley Civilisation commenced circa 3100 BC and comprised present-day northeast Afghanistan to Pakistan and northwest India.

Phoebe and Theia were upgrading and mentoring the scattered descendants of the Manus. They also introduced the beloved genetically engineered unicorn (ekazRGga in Sanskrit) into the Indus Valley. This beautiful creature appeared to be a small horse with pure white hair, blue eyes, cloven hooves and a long spiralled horn projecting from its forehead. Interestingly, at Mohenjo-daro and Harappa your archaeologists have unearthed stone seals each depicting a unicorn.

Many Hindu texts and Sanskrit epics describe flying palaces or chariots of the gods. In the Vedas there are descriptions of flying chariots employed by various star beings. In the Sanskrit epics they are called vimAnas (Sanskrit, 'traversing, palace, aerial vehicle').

Importantly, it was not just the Cyclopes being viewed in the heavens of the Indus Valley. An enormous golden spacecraft and smaller airships also started visiting the Indus Valley circa 2900 BC. The Pleiadeans and Lyrans were no longer the only star beings on your planet.

A crew of radiant gods had descended to Earth.

* * *

Have you been wondering what happened to Jahsoes and Merope?

Let's refresh your memory.

In 4500 BC the Pleiadeans arrived on planet Earth. The team comprised: Atlas (leader); males Jahsoes, Quetzalcoatl and Viracocha; females Pleione, Merope, Electra, Maya, Celaeno, Alcyone, Taygete and Sterope.

After an extensive reconnaissance of the Atlantean Empire, and consultation with Cronus and Rhea, Atlas and Pleione made their home in Lower Itza.

Six of the sisters (Electra, Maya, Celaeno, Alcyone, Taygete and Sterope) had a very strong bond and chose to live together in the southern part of Atlantis near the smaller volcano (which they named Zaila PrIti or Mountain of Love). They adored water and spent much time teaching and playing in Avalon. The Seven Sisters (includes Merope) are masters of Magick.

Viracocha chose an inhabited island to the west of Atlantis. Quetzalcoatl negotiated dominion over Poseidia, a large inhabited island near present-day Bimini (also to the west of Atlantis). He subsequently renamed the island Sundara.

Jahsoes (pronounced Yah-sues) is the most spiritually advanced of all the Pleiadeans. That is his real name and its origins are obscure. His appearance is striking: pure white hair cascading over his shoulders, white eyebrows, eyelashes and moustache, with almond-shaped blue eyes (the only male of our crew to not have a beard). Jahsoes prefers solitude, spending his days in prayer, meditation and communion with the Source. He says his mission is to explore the depth and extent of Love. Merope is a virtuous female with shoulder-length white hair and almond-shaped blue eyes. Merope was enamoured by Jahsoes' pure energy resonance. She became his soul companion and star mate. She shared her knowledge of Magick. Jahsoes ushered her to serene preternatural existence.

Jahsoes and Merope chose to reside on the uninhabited island east of Atlantis (where the Manus had built NaukA before the cataclysm).

In 3100 BC the second cataclysm overwhelmed the Atlantean Empire. It started on the island of Sundara when the exceedingly overcharged Fire Stone exploded. The enormous excess energy was partially conducted to uncovered Fire Stones in the Atlantean Empire and to local power-inducing crystals. The effects were devastating. The Atlantis Fire Stone, Avalon Fire Stone and three other Fire Stones exploded. Most local power crystals also received an intense blast.

Sundara was obliterated and the entire island sank into the ocean, hauling all inhabitants and the temple to a watery grave. Viracocha's island, and numerous smaller islands, suffered the same fate. The combined forces of the Avalon and Atlantis Fire Stone explosions, and the geologically unstable Mid-Atlantic Ridge, caused a violent upheaval in Atlantis. The Atlantis land mass broke up into smaller islands. There were extensive casualties in the Atlantean Empire. The deceased included Lyran gods, Lyran children of the gods and the majority of Atlanteans.

At the time of the cataclysm, Jahsoes and Merope were engaged in a very deep meditation. They were suddenly woken by the forceful shock wave on Atlantis. There were no inhabitants on their island so they immediately 'jumped' across the Mediterranean Sea, arriving on the coast of present-day Israel.

Once everything had settled, the gods convened on the northwest coast of Africa (present-day Morocco) to discuss the strategy for Earth.

You will recall that the Cyclopes and sacred crystals were shared among the gods; then they dispersed to various locations on your planet. Their missions were similar: selective upgrading of local inhabitants' DNA and spreading the gifts of civilisation.

Although they telepathically communicated with the other Pleiadeans, Jahsoes and Merope did not attend the Morocco conference. They were on a different kind of mission. Their journey was inward, exploring the depths of Love, surfing the multi-dimensions, and treading the path of Light. They were not allocated an airship, a crew or sacred crystals.

Jahsoes and Merope loved the climate and landscape of Israel, and spent countless hours upon its shores, immersed in prayer, meditation and communion with the Source.

One morning, during a mindful stroll along an exquisite beach, they noticed a golden spacecraft and airships descending toward present-day Egypt. Their interest was piqued; it seemed that new star beings had arrived on the planet. They decided to visit the neighbouring country in the near future.

An intriguing thought flitted across Merope's mind: How would the next millennium on Earth unfold?

* * *

A race of star beings had been watching the developments on Earth for a very long time.

They lived in Earth's sun, which offered an interesting vantage point over the planets of your solar system.

Solars are 2-metre-tall humanoids, with glowing hairless bodies, golden skin, and luminous blue or green eyes. Their robust bodies last for 700 years and thrive in high temperatures. Other races often refer to them as the 'golden beings'.

What is the cultural signature of the Solars? Though not as advanced as the Arcturians, Lyrans and Pleiadeans, the Solars have mastered technology and space travel. Virtue and justice are supreme tenets of their ethical base. They value innovatory intelligence and acquisition of knowledge.

The crew that was despatched to Earth comprised: Ra (leader); males Amun, Thoth, Osiris, Shu, Seth and Geb; females Tefnut, Isis, Hathor, Nephthys and Nut.

The motivation for their expedition was not the recent cataclysm; rather, they had observed the dispersing of the Pleiadeans across the planet and surmised that advanced star beings were finally ready to share their knowledge. It seemed to be a fortuitous opportunity.

Ra means 'sun' or 'creative power'. Ra is an imposing figure: tall, glowing, bald-headed, with luminous blue eyes. He is authoritative, brusque and commanding. He carries the silver-white Staff of Light, which has two serpents intertwined along it and a pine cone at the top. This magical staff focuses the light. As Ra states: 'Light can be used as a weapon; it can be used to communicate with other realms; and it can open the consciousness to the multi-dimensions.'

His crew are multi-disciplined; however, certain 'sun-gods' have critical functions.

Tefnut is the protector and defender of Ra. She is known as the Lady of Flame and Eye of Ra. Her all-seeing eye perceives everything, everywhere, in every dimension. She has the unique ability to manifest in a non-humanoid form, allowing her to wander discreetly and unobtrusively.

Amun is known as the 'hidden one' because he is capable of rendering himself invisible. This useful trait allows him to maintain a low profile (which Ra prefers for his crucial Solars). Amun's gift is the ability to join with and amplify another sun-god's energy, thereby creating a supernova power or explosion of light. That explosion can be graded to produce various defensive mechanisms, from temporary blindness to searing heat. Amun usually only links with Ra, resulting in a combined force called Amun-Ra.

Thoth possesses a supreme intelligence. He is assigned to acquire, record and protect sacred knowledge. As with Amun, Ra endeavours to keep him inconspicuous. He is deliberately set aside from conflict or wars to ensure the security of sacred information. Thoth invented and introduced hieroglyphic writing into ancient Egypt, partly as a means to cryptically obscure advanced knowledge.

In 2900 BC Ra and his crew hovered over Egypt. They finally descended upon Lunu (later renamed Heliopolis or 'City of the Sun') located at the beginning of the Nile Delta in Lower Egypt (Northern Egypt).

The arrival of foreign star beings attracted the immediate attention of Atlas and Pleione. With Cronus retired they were the leaders of planet Earth. Also, they were already working in North Africa, Egypt and the Indus Valley.

Ra knew the cultural signature of the Pleiadeans: They are the lovers and spiritual teachers of the galaxy; characterised as mystical, wise, virtuous, peaceful and kind. He perceived no threat or potential conflict. He surmised that honesty and gentle communication would be the way forward.

At the initial meeting with Atlas and Pleione, he immediately made clear the motivation of their expedition. He also offered access to all their knowledge and technology, a strategic overture which engendered trust from the Pleiadeans. Uncharacteristically, Ra introduced Thoth and proposed that the Pleiadeans avail themselves of all the sacred information.

It was a brilliant start to a mutually beneficial and fulfilling relationship.

Ra had observed the developments in the Americas, the United Kingdom, Mediterranean Europe and North Africa. Those areas were already under dominion of the Pleiadeans. He requested permission to settle the sun-gods in suitably hot and fertile Egypt, and to invest advanced knowledge into Egypt and countries to the east (where there was less Pleiadean activity).

Atlas and Pleione found those terms agreeable.

Pleione was spending the majority of her time assisting the six sisters in the United Kingdom and Mediterranean Europe, and she was teaching in the Indus Valley.

Atlas decided to work closely with Ra and Thoth. It made sense to monitor and measure their knowledge, ethics and strategy. Thoth was invited to interact with the Pleiadean-Atlantean crew. Over the next few years, true to their word, Ra and Thoth shared all their knowledge and technology.

With trust firmly cemented between the two leaders, Thoth was allowed to apply his formidable intellect and study the Lyran/Pleiadean sacred crystals. That opened up a whole new level of sacred information to the Solars. In time, Thoth became known as the 'sage of the sun-gods'.

Atlas and Pleione were responsible for the initial selective upgrading of local inhabitants' DNA and gradual dissemination of the gifts of civilisation in Egypt and the Indus Valley circa 3100 BC. The Nile Valley, originally inhabited by scattered hunter-gatherers and fishermen, underwent rapid socio-cultural evolution. The Indus Valley progressed in a similar way. Phoebe and Theia were visiting many countries, including Mesopotamia, to upgrade and teach the descendants of the Manus (members of secret societies and mystery schools) circa 3100 BC.

From circa 2900 BC the Solars began sharing advanced teachings in Egypt, the Indus Valley and Mesopotamia (Mesopotamia corresponds roughly to most of present-day Iraq, plus Kuwait, the eastern parts of Syria and south-eastern Turkey). Those areas strongly benefitted from the gifts of civilisation and introduction of writing by the Pleiadeans, Lyrans and Solars, which cultivated an erudite and esoteric cultural archetype.

A side note for ancient historians: The dispersion of Pleiadeans (and Pleiadean-Atlanteans), and the subsequent arrival of Solars, explains your present-day archaeologists' reports of the 'unaccountable' birth of civilisation in many parts of the world. This includes Egypt's First Dynasty circa 3100 BC; Indus Valley Civilisation circa 3100 BC (present-day northeast Afghanistan to Pakistan and northwest India); Sumer, Mesopotamia circa

3100 BC (present-day southern Iraq); the founding of Troy circa 3000 BC (present-day Anatolia, Turkey); England's megalithic site at Stonehenge and sacred stone circles at Avebury circa 3000 BC; Scotland's Standing Stones of Stenness circa 3100 BC; Caral, Peru circa 3050 BC (near present-day Lima); and Mesoamerica's Maya Long Count calendar which began in 3114 BC. Many of those civilisations sprang up 'mature' with no evident archaic period.

* * *

Everything was progressing satisfactorily on Earth.

3100 BC was the beginning of a new phase of widespread civilisation on your planet. This was enhanced by the arrival of the sun-gods in 2900 BC.

As always in life, nothing stays the same. There is that element of rogue unpredictability which causes you to throw hands up in exasperation.

All you can do is take a deep breath, analyse the situation, create a novel strategy, adapt, and move forward. A sense of humour certainly helps. (I am smiling now.)

Five decades after the Solars arrived, we noticed a large cigar-shaped spacecraft and eleven saucer-shaped airships surveying the planet. We sensed the unusual energy fields and decided to keep to ourselves. Pleiadeans are not violent; we are not warriors. We are a peaceful race who can simply 'jump' away from conflict and reside in another dimension. In fact, we have the power to shift our home planets and stars to other dimensions too.

The visiting star beings must have noticed the congregation of Solar spacecraft in Egypt. They probably assumed that Egypt was the centre of political and administrative power. (The Cyclopes were scattered around the rest of the planet.)

They landed in Lunu and approached the colossal Temple of Ra. Up the shimmering steps and into the huge courtyard sprinkled with imposing statues and towering obelisks. Then ushered into the immense hall with marble pillars standing like sentries guarding each side.

Unknown to the Solars, Lyrans and Pleiadeans, the crew comprised a Reptilian named Apophis (leader) and eleven Greys. Apophis (originally known as Apep) was a practitioner of the dark arts. His natural form was that of a tall lizard but he was also a master shape-shifter.

You are going to need a brief flashback. Let's go way back.

After the Elohim had created physical life on stars and planets, they let Natural Law take its course. They kept a watchful eye on the protracted evolutionary process, noting with fascination the development of multifarious physical species. Eventually humanoid races began to emerge on a few planets. The Elohim chose to strategically enhance their DNA and observe the ramifications.

That intervention created rapidly advancing races in the Lyra and Boötes constellations of our galaxy, home of the Lyrans and Arcturians.

Over millennia the Lyrans developed into a highly advanced race who mastered genetics, technology, clean and free energy, propulsion systems, space travel, artificial intelligence (AI) and other scientific disciplines. Gradually they spread to other planets in the Lyra star system. Peace and harmony prevailed in their worlds.

Every race becomes defined by a cultural signature. At heart, the Lyrans are scientists, explorers, experimenters and observers.

They are characterised as academic, dispassionate, contemplative and tranquil.

Arcturus of the Boötes constellation is the brightest star in Earth's Northern Celestial Hemisphere and fourth brightest star in the night sky, after Sirius, Canopus and Alpha Centauri. Arcturus is about 180 times more luminous than your sun. All beings of this race are called Arcturians, after their sacred star; however, they inhabit many planets in their star system.

The principal planet is Mani, which means 'jewel', a glowing orb graced with tree-lined mountains, lush forests, sparkling rivers and gleaming oceans. The northernmost point of this planet hosts both the Pagoda, an enormous multi-tiered building housing the Planetary Government, and the crystal Temple of Arcturus, home of the Galactic Government. The highest level of the Galactic Government comprises ten Supreme Galactic Leaders, one secretive Time Lord, and a Light Seer linked to the Universal Council of Light.

Arcturus is exceptionally peaceful, free of even the slightest traces of poverty, crime and violence. Weapons are banned on all their planets and are only utilised by the Galactic Military to protect technologically weaker races from exploitation, enslavement or annihilation.

What is the cultural signature of the Arcturians? They are the leaders and protectors of the galaxy. Characterised as wise, virtuous and just. They prefer not to intervene in the internal affairs or evolution of other races. The motto 'Interference is Perilous' is their guiding light, a piece of wisdom accrued from millennia of experience.

Unfortunately, a third advanced race had developed in a distant galaxy. The 2.5-metre-tall humanoid Reptilians. Similar to the Lyrans, they became master geneticists and space explorers. However, their cultural signature is aggressive domination. They are characterised as highly cognitive, deceptive, controlling and arrogant.

Long-lasting galactic wars erupted between the Lyrans and Reptilians. Two events shifted the security of our galaxy. The Arcturians, who steadfastly refused to engage in violence, had become the most technologically advanced beings in the Milky Way. Secondly, the Reptilians threatened the planet Mani. After the Cosmic War, and defeat of the Lizard beings, the Arcturians created the Galactic Federation to lead and protect the races of our galaxy.

The vast majority of star beings are benevolent and peaceable. Shared technology and united forces of the Galactic Federation inhibit the Reptilians and rogue star beings. The Federation also protects primitive planets and species.

That's the end of your flashback.

Ra appeared in the immense hall, carrying his powerful Staff of Light. Nine sun-gods stood by his side. (Amun rendered himself invisible and Thoth was kept hidden.)

Apep had cunningly shape-shifted into a 2-metre-tall golden-skinned humanoid. He introduced his crew of eleven lab-cloned Greys (who were each 1.2 metres tall, and appeared docile and harmless).

A subtle mind-probe had yielded sufficient facts to generate an appropriate strategy. Apep said he was a star traveller interested in exploring foreign worlds. In exchange for allowing him to stay on Earth, he offered Ra complete access to his knowledge and technology. He also proposed to spread advanced teachings throughout Egypt and other countries under Ra's jurisdiction.

Ra quietly consulted with Atlas, Pleione, Phoebe and Theia. He noticed the strange wariness among his compatriots. They agreed that the new star beings could stay on the planet, on condition that Ra was responsible for the 'project' and the Pleiadeans and Lyrans were left alone.

In 2850 BC Apep and the Greys took up residence on Earth.

The Solars were never really sure about the motives of Apep. In unguarded moments he let slip that he was looking for someone, perhaps an age-old adversary. At other times, he seemed keen to acquire power and technology. He became intrigued by the history of the Atlantean Empire and the residual Islands of Atlantis.

As the years passed, Apep gradually earned Ra's trust.

However, because of a strange warning from a pair of time-travelling Arcturians (read the book 5D) and a prophecy from the visionary Isis (read the books 5D and Star Child), Ra proceeded with caution. He kept the sun-gods Amun and Thoth concealed, and he shared limited knowledge and technology with Apep.

Within a decade the true face of Apep emerged. It became clear that he enjoyed power. Apep and his entourage began systematically oppressing and dominating the native population. He renamed himself Apophis, proclaimed himself the god of darkness, and demanded that he be worshipped. He regularly shape-shifted into his natural form of a 2.5-metre-tall lizard, earning him the epithet Dark Lizard or Evil Lizard.

In a sudden grab for power and advanced technology, Apophis initiated a calculated and coordinated attack against the Solars.

A war in the heavens ensued. The battle was waged across Egypt, Mesopotamia and the Indus Valley (creating the cultural myths about flying chariots, airships and a war of the gods). Ra's superior technology ensured that most of Apophis' spacecraft were destroyed. However, three key events occurred before

Apophis and five remaining Grey airships escaped into hyperspace.

Ra discovered the identity of retired Cronus and, in an effort to protect his life, summoned him to the temple just prior to the horrendous battle. The timing was unfortunate. Unbeknown to Cronus his death was imminent. You will recall that Lyrans can choose when to die and how to move forward. If they prefer not to transcend to a higher spiritual dimension upon death, they can simply transfer their consciousness to a newly created physical body. Cronus had done that numerous times.

When the blasts rained from the sky onto the Temple of Ra, Cronus had neither time nor technology on his side. As his wounded body collapsed he made a split-second decision. Notwithstanding that it is regarded as unethical, upon physical death Lyrans can transfer their consciousness to another living being in close proximity. Upon entering this 'vehicle' they can repress the host's consciousness and take control of the body. Usually this is only a temporary measure enacted in an emergency. No harm is done to the host. Cronus transferred his consciousness and survived. This event formed part of the evolution of Cronus into a hardened strategic warrior.

Realising that Apophis was a Reptilian, and immediately suspecting his true motives, Phoebe and Theia (each with a Cyclops and Pleiadean-Atlantean crew) entered into the battle. Apophis targeted them and deftly annihilated both spacecraft. Also deceased were the remaining four Lyran children of the gods.

The Solars were embroiled in a defensive battle against Apophis; they failed to notice the lone Grey airship heading toward the Islands of Atlantis. It had one mission: blast the two Fire Stones and destroy the original Lyran experiment. Cronus' old Pleiadean-Atlantean crew rushed to intercept but were too late. The Grey airship was obliterated but the cataclysmic explosion of the Fire

Stones, compounded by the geologically unstable Mid-Atlantic Ridge, caused a final violent upheaval. The Islands of Atlantis collapsed into the sea, dragging every Atlantean to a watery grave.

It was the end of the Lyran dream.

* * *

Grieving is a natural process that takes its own time.

Amid the sorrowful atmosphere, the gods convened in Egypt.

The Solars were scathed and scarred but none were deceased. It was a tough learning experience.

The Lyrans had only one land-based survivor: Cronus (no longer in a Lyran body). Oceanus and Tethys and a multitude of nymphs lived serenely underwater.

The Pleiadeans had not been involved in the battle. They extended their condolences to the star beings.

Despite the sadness, there were no accusations or recriminations. There was no blame to be assigned. Everyone had operated with virtuous intention. When Life throws an unexpected wobble, you have to practice acceptance, hold hands, talk about it and move forward.

There would be a time of stillness and inactivity. A period of mourning.

A commemoration of the magnificent Atlantean Empire.

When the star beings felt ready, the anthropological upgrades and teachings would recommence across the planet.

Atlas and Pleione (each with their own Cyclops and eleven-member Pleiadean-Atlantean crew) would continue their mission in North Africa, Egypt and the Indus Valley. Pleione would spend most of her time with the six sisters in the United Kingdom and Mediterranean Europe, plus disseminate teachings in the Indus Valley. She took one Communication Stone, one Knowledge Stone, one Healing Stone, one Spirit Stone. Atlas decided to work closely with Ra and Thoth in Egypt, Mesopotamia and the Indus Valley. He took one Fire Stone, one Communication Stone, one Knowledge Stone, one Healing Stone, one Spirit Stone.

Electra, Maya, Celaeno, Alcyone, Taygete and Sterope would continue to spread the advanced teachings throughout the United Kingdom and Mediterranean Europe. Each of the two Cyclopes carried three sisters with an eleven-member Pleiadean-Atlantean crew. They possessed two Communication Stones, two Knowledge Stones, two Healing Stones, two Spirit Stones.

Viracocha still had a Cyclops and eleven-member Pleiadean-Atlantean crew. He would continue to work in South America. He owned one Fire Stone, one Communication Stone, one Knowledge Stone, one Healing Stone, one Spirit Stone.

Quetzalcoatl also had a Cyclops and eleven-member Pleiadean-Atlantean crew. He would continue his work in North America and Mesoamerica. He owned one Fire Stone, one Communication Stone, one Knowledge Stone, one Healing Stone, one Spirit Stone.

With the demise of Phoebe, Theia and the Lyran children of the gods (and their Pleiadean-Atlantean crews) the sacred crystals, which had been left with the Manus for safe keeping prior to the battle with Apophis, remained concealed in the mystery schools and secret societies. This totalled one Fire Stone, two Communication Stones, two Knowledge Stones, two Healing Stones, two Spirit Stones.

You will recall that after Iapetus' death, Cronus left Atlantis and bequeathed to his Pleiadean-Atlantean crew the Cyclops and two

Fire Stones, two Communication Stones, two Knowledge Stones, two Healing Stones, two Spirit Stones. (Those two Fire Stones were destroyed by the Grey airship, precipitating the final Atlantean cataclysm.) Cronus had retained one Communication Stone, one Knowledge Stone, one Healing Stone, one Spirit Stone.

Cronus (no longer in a Lyran body) summoned his Pleiadean-Atlantean crew. He decided to work with Atlas, Ra and Thoth in Egypt, Mesopotamia and the Indus Valley. He therefore now controlled three Communication Stones, three Knowledge Stones, three Healing Stones, three Spirit Stones.

In case you've been counting:

Cyclopes remaining: 7

Sacred crystals remaining: 4 Fire Stones, 11 Communication Stones, 11 Knowledge Stones, 11 Healing Stones, 11 Spirit Stones.

* * *

By 2800 BC things were running smoothly on Earth.

Apart from occasional communication and meetings with other Pleiadeans, Viracocha and Quetzalcoatl focused on their work in the Americas. As always, they employed intermittent, cautious and selective upgrading of local hunter-gatherers' DNA along with slow and steady dissemination of the gifts of civilisation (agriculture, mathematics, physics, architecture, engineering, astronomy, meteorology, geology, social organisation, government and a moral code).

Pleione and the six sisters (Electra, Maya, Celaeno, Alcyone, Taygete, Sterope) kept to themselves too. Their strong bond formed a Sisterhood, a consciousness that seeped into their teachings in the United Kingdom, Mediterranean Europe and the Indus Valley. The Sisterhood consciousness, combined with the Pleiadean values of virtue, responsibility, compassion, loving-kindness and peace, cultivated an exquisite cultural archetype. Similar to their brothers in the Americas, Pleione and the six sisters became renowned for healing the sick (by utilising the sacred crystals).

Atlas, Ra and Thoth shared all their information, knowledge and technology. Amun and Tefnut remained near Ra, although mostly relatively inconspicuous (Amun preferred being invisible and Tefnut favoured her non-humanoid form). Cronus, with the assistance of his Pleiadean-Atlanteans, transferred his consciousness to a newly created Lyran physical body. This motley crew of star beings (Atlas, Ra, Thoth, Amun, Tefnut, Cronus) formed the elite leadership of Egypt, residing in Lunu (later renamed Heliopolis or 'City of the Sun') which is located at the beginning of the Nile Delta in Lower Egypt (Northern Egypt). Together they controlled one Fire Stone, four Communication Stones, four Knowledge Stones, four Healing Stones, four Spirit Stones.

Ra gave dominion of Upper Egypt (Southern Egypt) to Osiris and Isis; then despatched the remaining sun-gods (Shu, Seth, Geb, Hathor, Nephthys, Nut) to spread advanced knowledge into the countries east of Egypt, including Mesopotamia and the Indus Valley.

In 2700 BC Thoth contrived the building of pyramids. The primary intention was to store sacred information and knowledge. Later the elite leaders of Egypt would also be buried within these sacrosanct structures.

In 2650 BC Thoth, Amun, Ra and Atlas (with Pleiadean-Atlantean crews) built the first Pyramid of Djoser about 30 km south of Heliopolis (20 km south of present-day Cairo). This was followed circa 2550-2450 BC by the Pyramid of Khufu (Hellenised as 'Cheops') aka the Great Pyramid of Giza, the Pyramid of Khafre (Hellenised as 'Chephren') and the Pyramid of Menkaure (Hellenised as 'Mykerinos') located together about 15 km southwest of present-day Cairo, Northern Egypt.

You will recall that Jahsoes and Merope were on a different kind of mission. Their journey was inward, exploring the depths of Love, surfing the multi-dimensions, and treading the path of Light. Jahsoes and Merope loved the climate and landscape of Israel, and spent countless hours upon its shores, immersed in prayer, meditation and communion with the Source.

They had witnessed the initial descent of the Solars in 2900 BC. Their interest was piqued and they decided to visit the neighbouring country in the near future. Jahsoes and Merope considered 'time' a meaningless concept; instead they lived in a surrendered state of divine flow. Hence, more than 400 years passed before they finally 'jumped' to Egypt to meet the Solars.

In 2500 BC Jahsoes and Merope arrived at the Temple of Ra in Lunu. The sun-gods had long been anticipating this meeting and graciously welcomed them. The Solars could sense the extraordinary energy emanating from these Pleiadeans. Curiously, the sun-gods' carefully tailored questions were met either by abstruse answers or serene silence.

Thoth was intrigued by these reclusive preternatural beings. At the instigation of Atlas, Thoth handed a set of the sacred crystals to Jahsoes and Merope. It was the first time they had encountered the Lyran crystals. They promptly shaped their hands into the holy symbol (making a circle of thumb and index finger, by placing tip of index finger just inside tip of thumb, and fully extending the other three close-together fingers) and hovered them over the Fire Stone, Communication Stone, Knowledge Stone, Healing Stone and Spirit Stone.

Much to the consternation and confusion of Thoth, within one hour Jahsoes and Merope absorbed the knowledge and consciousness of the sacred crystals. To prove it, Jahsoes raised his hand into the transmission symbol (palm facing forward; thumb and four close-together fingers fully extending and pointing upward) and healed a sick man laying outside the temple.

Still uncertain about what had occurred, Thoth begged for an explanation.

Jahsoes gazed at him compassionately, flared his hand and stated: 'Magick is the science and art of manifestation in conformity with Will and Intent. Thumb is Fire (solar plexus chakra), Index Finger is Air (heart chakra), Middle Finger is Aether (throat chakra), Ring Finger is Earth (base or root chakra), Baby Finger is Water (sacral chakra).'

Mystified, Thoth glanced at Atlas.

Atlas shrugged.

After consultation with Atlas, Ra and Cronus, Jahsoes and Merope decided to stay in Egypt and share elementary mystical teachings.

The most spiritually advanced of all the Pleiadeans flowed among the Solars, Cronus, and his fellow star beings. They struggled to comprehend the deeper lessons; however, they gradually transitioned deeper into Love and shifted toward the Light.

Merope and Tefnut soon forged a close relationship and would disappear for days. Merope (who adored the sea) also visited Oceanus and Tethys to share the secrets of Magick.

From 2050 BC Thoth, Amun, Osiris, Isis and Jahsoes (with Pleiadean-Atlantean crews) built the magnificent Karnak Temple;

and from 1400 BC they built the spectacular Luxor Temple. Both are located in present-day Luxor, Southern Egypt.

Over the next millennium, advanced knowledge, mystical teachings and sacred information swirled through the upper echelons of present-day Egypt, Israel, Jordan, Mesopotamia and the Indus Valley. It also cascaded into the elite leadership positioned across the rest of your planet.

At the same time, the next phase of learning from the anthropological experiment was unfolding. It would lead to intriguing questions about the nature of humans and even more interesting decisions pertaining to the future of Earth.

* * *

In 500 BC the gods convened at the Temple of Ra in Egypt.

All the Pleiadeans and Solars and Cronus were present. Oceanus and Tethys remained in their underwater paradise but connected telepathically to the land-based Lyran.

The topic for discussion was the anthropological experiment. A number of issues had been raised.

There were various tiers of humans on Earth.

The most advanced (and relatively scarce) was the *Homo luminous* (Latin, 'human', 'light') which resulted from the insertion of Pleiadean and Lyran DNA into the human genome, and modification of specific genes, sparking a transition from *Homo sapiens* (Latin, 'human', 'wisdom'). Insertion of high-resonance DNA can result in disorientation, confusion and a period of adjustment for the organism. Initial, and often long-term, effects may include: a sense of not belonging to your tribe or culture;

questions of identity and purpose; a hunger for advanced knowledge; awakening of consciousness; and ascension to a higher dimension. Those beings often struggled to stay on Earth and were eventually moved to another world or dimension.

The *Homo luminous* or Pleiadean-Atlanteans were tall, slender and highly intelligent, with skin of varying colour (originating from different continents), auburn or blonde hair, and green or blue eyes. The Pleiadeans provided advanced knowledge and helped them develop their innate clairvoyance, telepathy and telekinesis. In time, the Pleiadean-Atlanteans naturally gravitated to leadership positions.

The more common upgrade resulted from insertion of Lyran DNA into the human genome, and modification of specific genes. This created a superior *Homo sapiens* which the star beings designated as Atlanteans (even after the final cataclysm of Atlantis). Atlanteans had various skin and hair colour (originating from different continents), blue eyes, supreme health and long life. The life span of Atlanteans ranged from 300-400 years, some living as long as 500 years.

Then there were the regular *Homo sapiens* or non-upgraded humans.

Atlanteans and regular humans were progressively given the gifts of civilisation (agriculture, mathematics, physics, architecture, engineering, astronomy, meteorology, geology, social organisation, government and a moral code) and slowly transitioned from a lifestyle of nomadic hunter-gathering to one of agriculture and settlement.

The one issue that cropped up frequently was the disparity among the various tiers of humans. Each possessed different levels of intelligence and innate characteristics. Even with superlative role modelling and transmission of ethical codes there arose egotism and jealousy. It seemed that humans always desired more knowledge, resources, abilities and power.

As you have witnessed, when knowledge, resources, abilities and power are not balanced by spiritual and emotional maturity, disaster is inevitable. This is probably the greatest lesson garnered from your planet's ancient history.

A contrary but similar issue was the elite leadership on Earth.

Star beings are seen as 'gods' by humans. It is also the nature of advanced beings to lead and rule. Even when star beings (or Pleiadean-Atlanteans) tried to maintain a low profile and blend with the local population, they often landed up being revered or worshipped. Unfortunately, godly kings, rulers and priests often created disempowered and dependent peoples who no longer embraced autonomy and responsibility nor progressed spiritually.

The fundamental question related to those issues: What is the best way for humans to advance spiritually, cognitively and emotionally?

After lengthy and spirited debate, we agreed on a Master Plan: Halt all upgrading of humans' DNA. Cease all teachings. Gradually withdraw from positions of authority and leadership. Encourage humans to take responsibility for themselves and autonomously determine their own destiny.

We had to accept that divine genetics would gradually be bred out, and human physiology would steadily regress.

This plan would take much courage from the star beings. In a sense, humans were in an adolescent phase, and we had to grant them more freedom, decision-making and autonomy. We would, however, continue to act as role models and counsellors, using a light touch to inspire and guide humankind.

During the ensuing centuries we noted the rising and strengthening of the human spirit. We had to take a step back, breathe deeply and watch our children grow up. Often there were concerns regarding egotism, greed, aggression, violence and power. We walked a narrow path between independence and interference. We countered sporadic resentment about our withdrawal with benevolent mentorship.

It seemed the next phase of the anthropological experiment was flourishing.

* * *

In 50 BC the gods convened on a shore of Israel.

Jahsoes and Merope had recently returned to their beloved home.

On the table for discussion was the final phase of the anthropological experiment. It was a natural and inevitable extension of the Master Plan.

The gods believed it was time to withdraw completely from Earth and leave humankind to construct their own future.

They knew this 'ultimate solution' carried inherent rewards and risks.

Although the Solars were fully committed to leaving, the remaining Lyrans refused to leave their cherished experiment. It was against their tenets and philosophy to abandon the 'project'. Most of the Pleiadeans and Pleiadean-Atlanteans pledged to depart with the Solars.

Every decision was motivated by the same fundamental question: What is the best way for humans to advance spiritually, cognitively and emotionally?

To countervail the absence of the gods, the star beings agreed to initiate an almighty spiritual inspiration. A final powerful transmission of high-resonance ethics and values.

Jahsoes and Merope, with a crew of advanced beings, would travel the Earth and share their mystical teachings about Love and Light.

The crew comprised Cronus, six of his Pleiadean-Atlanteans and four Atlanteans. They would carry one Communication Stone, one Knowledge Stone, one Healing Stone, one Spirit Stone. A Cyclops would be retained for discreet use.

Near the end of the conference, Isis shared a prophecy: *Once the mission of Jahsoes and Merope is complete, the Earth will struggle in a battle of light and darkness. When enough humans awaken and rise up together, their collective light will overthrow the dark lattice. At that time, the Pleiadeans will return and Atlantis will rise.*

We agreed to cache the remaining sacred crystals in secret locations across your planet. I buried my sacred crystals in Yucatan. Viracocha buried his in Peru. Thoth buried his beneath the Great Sphinx of Giza. I may not reveal the rest of the locations.

Soon after the sacred crystals were hidden, the star beings departed from Earth.

* * *

The Pleiadeans stayed in telepathic contact with Jahsoes and Merope, emanating affectionate encouragement and monitoring their activities from afar.

Just prior to the commencement of the Love and Light Mission, a solitary entity landed in Israel. His name was Hades, remote commander of the original Sirian crew. You will recall that the Sirians were forbidden from returning to Earth. Perhaps he was sent to learn something; maybe it was a karmic opportunity.

Wherever Jahsoes and Merope journeyed, he followed. He tried to ingratiate himself with the crew. Cronus treated him with disdain. When later (misogynous) myths proclaimed Jahsoes and his 'twelve disciples', Merope was invariably replaced by Hades. Did Hades serve the darkness? Was he a tempter or betrayer? Was he sent to challenge the depths of Love?

Jahsoes ('Jay' to his companions), Merope and the crew travelled across the planet for more than seven decades. They shared the sacred Pleiadean values (virtue, responsibility, compassion, loving-kindness and peace), spread the mystical teachings, healed the sick, and performed 'miracles'. They serenely and joyfully fulfilled the Love and Light Mission.

Eventually they withdrew from your world too. Earth was fully surrendered to humankind. The star beings had invested much inspiration, knowledge and technology. The rest was up to you. A new era began on your planet.

* * *

Remember what I said in the very beginning?

'I am going to tell you a story. An ancient story. A magical history that will resonate in your soul. A history ingrained in your deepest consciousness, in your myths and mysteries. For many of you, it will explain your innermost feelings, longings, reveries and dreams. For some of you, it may evoke a profound and beautiful déjà vu.'

I wonder which beings resonated with your soul ... I wonder if you remember your incarnation in the Atlantean Empire ... I wonder who you were and what role you played ... I wonder if you recall the advanced teachings ... I wonder if you dream of gliding serenely in the ocean ... or dancing with unicorns upon the islands ... or flying airships across an azure sky ... I wonder if your soul yearns for Lyra or Arcturus or the Pleiades or another resplendent star system?

As I leave you now ... contemplate your journey ... weaving through lifetimes ... playing in the multi-dimensions ... exploring the depths of Love ... walking the path of Light ... moving closer to the Source ... finding your way Home.

The star beings are destined to return to Earth.

I look forward to seeing you again.

Stephen Shaw's Books

Visit the website: www.i-am-stephen-shaw.com

I Am contains spiritual and mystical teachings from enlightened masters that point the way to love, peace, bliss, freedom and spiritual awakening.

Heart Song takes you on a mystical adventure into creating your reality and manifesting your dreams, and reveals the secrets to attaining a fulfilled and joyful life.

They Walk Among Us is a love story spanning two realities. Explore the mystery of the angels. Discover the secrets of Love Whispering.

The Other Side explores the most fundamental question in each reality. What happens when the physical body dies? Where do you go? Expand your awareness. Journey deep into the Mystery.

Reflections offers mystical words for guidance, meditation and contemplation. Open the book anywhere and unwrap your daily inspiration.

5D is the Fifth Dimension. Discover ethereal doorways hidden in the fabric of space-time. Seek the advanced mystical teachings.

Star Child offers an exciting glimpse into the future on earth. The return of the gods and the advanced mystical teachings. And the ultimate battle of light versus darkness.

The Tribe expounds the joyful creation of new Earth. What happened after the legendary battle of Machu Picchu? What is Christ consciousness? What is Ecstatic Tantra?

The Fractal Key reveals the secrets of the shamans. This handbook for psychonauts discloses the techniques and practices used in psychedelic healing and transcendent journeys.

Stephen Shaw's Books

Atlantis illuminates the Star Beings and Earth's Ancient History. A magical history ingrained in your deepest consciousness, in your myths and mysteries. Discover the secret teachings of the star beings.

CPSIA information can be obtained
at www.ICGtesting.com
Printed in the USA
BVOW11s1813230417
482042BV00015B/334/P